# A SOURCEBOOK
## for
# STEWARDSHIP SERMONS

# A SOURCEBOOK
## for
# STEWARDSHIP SERMONS

by
JAMES E. CARTER

BAKER BOOK HOUSE       Grand Rapids, Michigan

ISBN: 0-8010-2339-4
Copyright © 1972 by Baker Book House Company
Printed in the United States of America

*Dedicated
to my parents,
the late Edward F. Carter
and Mrs. Sue Reaves Carter,
who first taught me the meaning of Christian Stewardship*

# INTRODUCTION

In presenting the full message of the Bible to modern man stewardship cannot be omitted. In both a presentation of the message and an observance of annual emphases the pastor is faced with the necessity of preparing stewardship messages.

At times material for these messages is hard to find. A germinal idea, an apt quotation, an interesting story, another sermon may be just what is needed to start a message on its way. These things this collection seeks to provide.

The material for this book came from the heat of a pastor's study. Through several years of sermonic preparation these materials have been gathered. They have now been compiled and put together in this volume as a ready reference for other pastors to use in preparation of stewardship sermons. It does not claim to be a complete book on Christian stewardship. It does purport to be a sourcebook containing sermons, stories, and sayings about one specialized area of Christian concern—stewardship.

My conception of Christian stewardship is that it is the total response of the individual to the grace of God. Stewardship involves money, but it is more than money: it is the self. All that we are, as well as all that we have, has been entrusted to us by God. How we use this is our stewardship. I have sought to convey this conviction in this book.

The contents of this work have come from many sources. I have tried to identify these sources as completely as possible. I am sorry if I have erred on any of them.

Mrs. Ola Clinton has prepared the typescript. For her help and the sharp eye of her husband, Dr. T. A. Clinton, who proofed the material I am grateful.

I trust that this sourcebook shall prove helpful to pastors, and informative, instructional, and edifying to the church members who will be the ultimate recipients of them.

JAMES E. CARTER

*Pastor's Study*
*First Baptist Church*
*Natchitoches, Louisiana*

# CONTENTS

# PART I
# SOME STEWARDSHIP SERMONS

# THE FELLOWSHIP OF CHRISTIAN GIVING

*II Corinthians 8:1-15*

*Fellowship* is a term that we use a great deal. It is a good, useful term. But when it comes to precise definition it is a somewhat elusive term. We use it to express that warm feeling of acceptance and give-and-take and the sheer enjoyment of being together. We use it to express a mutual interest. We use it to express a bond of unity that can reach across certain barriers.

It is in this latter respect that we can talk about a fellowship of Christian giving. In II Corinthians 8-9 attention is given to an offering Paul had been promoting. He had been asking the Gentile churches in the area of his missionary journeys to give a sum of money for the relief of the poor at Jerusalem. His concern was twofold: to give material substance to those in need and to bring about a happier relationship between Jewish and Gentile Christians. He thus sought to cultivate a fellowship of giving and receiving.

Now the Corinthian Christians had been lagging behind somewhat on this project. They had the desire. And apparently they had made a start. But they had not followed through with it.

As an example to them Paul used the Macedonians. They had given and had given liberally. It was not that they could necessarily afford to give either. As a group they were not much better off financially than the crowd at Jerusalem. But they sought this opportunity as a ministry. They gave voluntarily. Out of their poverty they gave as an act of joy and as an expression of their response to the grace of God. They wanted to be a part of the fellowship of Christian giving.

The Macedonians serve as an example to us, too. This incident tells us something important about the fellowship of Christian giving.

# THE DYNAMIC: GRACE

The dynamic for the fellowship of Christian giving is grace. Paul made very clear the dynamic for giving—it was grace. He did not appeal to legalism. . . . He did not appeal to the profit motive . . . . He did not place giving on a bargaining basis with God. . . . He emphasized it as a matter of grace.

This must be our dynamic for giving to Christ and the church. It is in response to God's grace. It is in gratitude for the blessings we have received from God, not as an attempt to get more.

Mark how this motive is stressed. It is used as an example: ". . . the grace of God bestowed on the churches of Macedonia" (vs. 1). The churches of Macedonia had responded to the appeal. Their response is recognized as a manifestation of the grace of God. The grace of God had not only been seen in their salvation. It was also seen in their response to help other Christians in their privation and suffering.

Grace is used as a plea: ". . . see that ye abound in this grace also" (vs. 7). This church at Corinth was not without either grace or gifts. They had abounded in faith. Many were the times in that pagan atmosphere they had demonstrated faith. They had utterance. They were not afraid of speaking a word of verbal witness for the Lord. Neither were they lacking in knowledge. Through God's grace they had an understanding of the Christian faith. Since they had these aspects of God's grace as a part of their life and experience they should have yet another—the grace of giving.

Grace is used in the supreme example of what Christ has done for us on the cross. "For ye know the grace of our Lord Jesus Christ, that, though he was rich, yet for your sakes he became poor, that ye through his poverty might be rich" (vs. 9). The supreme example of grace is what God has done for us through Christ. That is unmitigated grace. Surely the example of the grace of God in Jesus Christ could inspire Christians to practice grace. As Christ gave, we are to give.

God's grace to us and our gratitude for it become the basis for Christian giving. Many years ago a wealthy student at Williams College was accused of defacing college property and was sent to see President Mark Hopkins. He came in arrogantly, took out his purse, and asked how much were the damages. This was too much for President Hopkins, who commanded the young man to sit down. "No man," said the president, "can pay for what he receives here. Can you pay for the sacrifice of Colonel Williams who founded the college? Can you pay for the half-paid professors who have remained here to teach when they could have gone elsewhere? Every student here is a charity case."[1] And so are we. The knowledge of that fact helps to supply the dynamic for giving. The dynamic is grace.

## THE ATMOSPHERE: JOY

The atmosphere of the fellowship of Christian giving is joy. Read verse 2 again and you will notice a reference to the "abundance of their joy." This joy came from giving.

There is a joy in sharing with another and helping to meet his need. Some of the finest moments in your life that can be recalled are moments when you shared with another. You may have shared time, concern, interest, information, or money. But you shared—and received a special kind of joy.

Joy results from knowing that you have helped to make some things possible that would not have been possible without your giving. The Jerusalem Christians were actually destitute. These gifts would make life possible for them. The gifts you have given may have made it possible for someone to have food . . . or clothing . . . or medical attention . . . or education . . . or salvation. These gifts may have created hope . . . faith . . . dedication . . . and joy. Surely this contributes to the joy that is the atmosphere of the fellowship of Christian giving.

Knowing that your priorities are proper gives you joy in giving. How a person spends his money indicates what he thinks is important.

Methodist Bishop Gerald Kennedy has an enlightening discussion of the priorities shown in giving in his book *Fresh Every Morning*. He surmised that if a stranger from another planet should suddenly land on our planet and look at the budgets of the nations, he would certainly come to the conclusion that we believe in death but not in life. He would see us spending billions of dollars for defense and for the development of instruments of destruction which are out of date almost before they can be manufactured. This stranger would see the people being heavily taxed to arm against some enemy, but he would find them too poor to spend adequately for schools, for hospitals, or for the clearance of slums. He would come to the conclusion that we had lost our confidence in life.

But then the bishop asks an interesting question about church budgets. "What does an examination of the church budget show? Is our money being spent primarily for housekeeping chores and providing the institution with comfort and convenience? How much are we spending for carrying the good news around the world? And just what are we doing in our local communities to make life better? It might be a very good idea for any church to take an objective look at its budget and find out just what it really believes in and what its program is supposed to accomplish."

So far as the individual is concerned, a look at his checkbook stubs would say more about him than his public confession of faith. No matter how unmaterialistic one might claim to be, the way he actually spends his money is probably the best indication of his faith. Back in 1924 a minister listed some news items and compared them with the church records. He noticed this in the paper: "Mr. and Mrs. B. left last night for New York, where they will attend the World Series. They will be gone about three weeks, during which time they will visit Niagara and other points of interest in that section." When he turned to his church records, he found this: "Mr. B. sent his check to the treasurer for $60 covering his annual contribution for the support of the church benevolences. Accompanying it was a note saying that he was sorry it had to be less than last year."[2]

When a person is faithful in Christian giving he has his priorities right. That in itself helps to create joy.

The atmosphere in the fellowship of Christian giving is not one of compulsion, of fear, of niggardliness, but one of joy. When a Christian cooperates with other Christians in carrying out the work of Christ it creates an atmosphere of joy.

## THE ATTITUDE: TOTALITY OF LIFE

The attitude in the fellowship of Christian giving involves the totality of life. The key is found in verse 5: "It was more than we could have hoped for! First they gave themselves to the Lord, and then, by God's will, they gave themselves to us as well" (TEV).

We must always keep this straight in any discussion of Christian stewardship. We are not just talking about money or about raising money. We are talking about the dedication of a life to God. When the life is totally dedicated to God the material resources that we have will be dedicated to Him too.

The totality of dedication is the beginning place for stewardship. Athletes often display this brand of dedication and shame Christians by their dedication.

Bill Glass, in his book *Get in the Game,* tells of the dedication of Raymond Berry.

> The greatest pass receiver in the history of pro football is Raymond Berry of the Baltimore Colts. He has already bettered Billy Howton's life time record of 503 catches with several years of football still to play [the book was written in 1965]. But Raymond Berry is not a man with exceptional ability; actually, Raymond has a lot of physical defects. Compared to other pass receivers he is slow. He has poor vision. He has knee problems. He's always had a bad back. He has everything in the world against his being the great football player that he is. In 1960, when I was still with Detroit, we were playing Baltimore; Raymond had a bad knee. At half time Yale Larry and our other defensive backs were complaining about Berry.
>
> "He's dragging that one leg and still he's killing us."
>
> He caught ten passes that day at half speed with a bad knee. He is the greatest receiver who ever lived—for one reason—because he has a singleness of purpose.
>
> "This one thing I do," says Raymond Berry, "I'm going to be the greatest pass receiver the world has ever known."
>
> Raymond and I are personal friends and I know

he would never make such a statement aloud; he's much too modest for that. He must have this sort of dedication in his heart, because he works when everybody else rests.

One year at the Pro-Bowl a friend of mine, who played on the Western division team with Berry said,

"Day after day when everyone else had gone in after the workout, I saw him coming back out. One day I decided that I would watch and see what he was doing. He looked peculiar because he had a net over one shoulder and a ladder over the other and about ten or fifteen little boys tagging along behind. I followed him back out on the practice field. I watched him as he used the ladder to drape the big net over the goal post. He used the goal post as a backstop and he stood in front of the goal post with the net draped over it. Then he had the little boys throw the ball to him. And they threw it to every conceivable position. They'd throw it at ankle height, and then knee height, and on up, and Berry did what he calls the clock drill. He caught the ball at every conceivable position and starting over, he caught the ball at every position going the other way. And then he began to run. He took his running exercises catching the ball at every possible angle."

My friend says that Berry does this almost every day after workout. It's amazing how dedicated Berry really is.[3]

And it's amazing the lack of dedication that Christians often show to God. With this kind of dedication—the kind that gives God the totality of life—stewardship comes into proper focus.

The attitude that governs the fellowship of Christian giving is totality. Giving is seen as a part of the totality of response to God.

The fellowship of Christian giving is a tremendously exciting fellowship. But it must be preceded by becoming a part of the Christian fellowship itself, by first giving oneself to Christ. This is where it starts.

[1] Gerald Kennedy, *Fresh Every Morning* (New York: Harper and Row, 1966), p. 19. Reprinted by permission of the publisher.

[2] *Ibid.,* pp. 151-152.

[3] Bill Glass, *Get in the Game* (Waco: Word Books, 1965), pp. 128-129. Reprinted by permission of the publisher.

# SOME KEY CONCEPTS
# IN CHRISTIAN STEWARDSHIP

*I Corinthians 4:1-2*

Like everything else education has changed. Back in the dark ages when I was in school we didn't worry too much about the concepts behind a fact, we just learned it. In geography, and that is called "social studies" these days, we just learned where Madagascar and Zanzibar were located and let it go at that. The multiplication tables were committed to memory, we didn't spend any time trying to figure out relationships and grouping numbers and all that. If you could just get it in your head that $2 \times 2 = 4$, and keep it there, you got along fine.

But now the children are being taught concepts. And they are required to give not only the facts, but also the concepts behind them—why these facts are so. It is good. It has resulted in a more informed bunch of kids with a lot more understanding of why certain things are as they are.

Perhaps we ought to do a little more depth work in the area of Christian faith and beliefs also. We have often pontificated about certain truths without going into much background about why these things are believed and practiced.

Take the matter of Christian stewardship, for instance. We have quoted I Corinthians 4:1-2 and said that we are to be stewards. We have explained that a steward is one who manages the affairs of others and then talked about how we ought to practice stewardship, how we ought to tithe, and perhaps even put a little pressure on people to be good stewards without going into the background very well, without explaining the concepts.

So now let us look at a few of the key concepts of Christian stewardship. These are some of the bases for our belief in stewardship and our teaching of stewardship.

# ACCOUNTABILITY

Acountability is one key concept in Christian stewardship. Remember, the basic meaning of a steward is one who handles the affairs of another.

We begin with the idea that all that we have really belongs to God. The psalmist said, "The earth is the Lord's and the fullness thereof, the world and they that dwell therein." Adam was to subdue and use the earth: he didn't own it.

It is God who gives us the strength and the ability to acquire all that we have in a material way. In one of his last speeches to the children of Israel before they crossed the River Jordan into the Promised Land Moses reminded them of this very fact (Deut. 8:17-18).

We need to be reminded of it often. It is easy for us to get what Helmut Thielicke calls "the master of the house" attitude.

These things being true—that all the world and everything in it belongs to God and that God strengthens us and enables us to get what we have—then we are accountable to God for how we use it.

A. A. Hyde, a millionaire of Mentholatum manufacturing fame, said he began tithing when he was a hundred thousand dollars in debt. He had been warned, like many others have, by covetous people whose selfish and avaricious spirit kept them in debt to men in their ambitious efforts to make money or enjoy luxuries. These un-Scriptural people cautioned Mr. Hyde that it was dishonest to give God a tenth of his increase or income while he was in debt. Unless a Christian honestly obeys the Scripture, "Owe no man any thing" (Rom. 13:8), who is there among us that could not keep himself always in debt and thereby never have to pay God anything? Mr. Hyde agreed with his un-Scriptural counselors until one day it dawned upon him that, "The earth is the Lord's, and the fulness thereof: the world, and they that dwell therein" (Ps. 24:1), which made God his first Creditor. From this moment forward Mr. Hyde began paying God first, and eventually all of the other creditors were paid in full.

We are accountable to God first of all. God it is who has provided us with all we have.

## DEPENDABILITY

If I am accountable to God, can God depend on me? Paul's assertion is that it is required of stewards that they be found faithful. The Revised Standard Version translates that "trustworthy." A trustworthy person is a dependable person. Dependability is another key concept in Christian stewardship.

But what is the motivation for dependability? It cannot be legalistic alone. It cannot simply be altruistic. It cannot just be emotional. It must be the response of love and gratitude to God.

Jesus reminded us in the Sermon on the Mount that we could not serve two masters. If God is truly our master, if we have really submitted to the Lordship of Jesus Christ, then we will be dependable because we love Him and want to serve Him.

Then how much does it take to be dependable? That is really putting the question in the wrong order. That is looking for a minimum standard for faithfulness and dependability. The question is really: how much can I give to the One who has given so much to me? I think the Bible teaches a tithe. This has Biblical precedent. If the Jews were commanded to tithe, surely in a response of love to God's grace we could at least do that much.

What is our view of ourselves? We think of ourselves as dependable, but how does God judge us?

How do others see you? One morning in 1888 Alfred B. Nobel, inventor of dynamite, the man who grew wealthy by producing weapons of destruction, awoke to read his own obituary! It seems that Alfred's brother had died, and a French reporter carelessly reported the death of the wrong brother!

Anyone would have been shaken. But to Alfred B. Nobel, the shock was overwhelming. He suddenly saw himself as others saw him—an amazing discovery that few persons make. He was to the world "the dynamite king," the industrialist who became rich from explosives. So far as the general public was concerned this was "the whole story" of Nobel's life. To the world he was quite simply a "merchant of death," and for that alone he would be remembered by men.

Horrified by his obituary, Nobel resolved to do something different with his life. He would will his fortune for prizes to those who have done the most for the cause of world peace. His last will and testament would express his life's ideals. The result was the Nobel Prize, one of the most valued prizes granted today.

## AVAILABILITY

Availability is yet another key concept for Christian stewardship. In the final analysis, then, our stewardship turns on our commitment to Christ.

If we are not available to God, if we are not willing to give ourselves to Him in faith and trust, then it is very unlikely that we will make our money available to Him or give our money to Him.

Stewardship without the self is not truly Christian stewardship. As far as I am concerned, stewardship must be placed in the context of our total commitment to Christ, it must involve all of life and not just money, and it must be as a response of love, trust, and faith.

To me one of the finest expressions of stewardship in all the Scripture is found in II Corinthians 8:5. W. Morris Ford, former pastor of the First Baptist Church, Longview, Texas, once made some very interesting remarks concerning this verse.

A pastor went to see a member about his stewardship. Although a man of means, the man was not helping support the church either with his gifts or his presence.

After a few introductory remarks the pastor told why he had come. Before he could continue, the member began to pour out a string of complaints about the church and specific members. Finally, the man concluded, "All you want is my money!"

Sure that he had delivered a death blow, he was quite startled when the pastor said, "Yes, that's about all you have that the Lord can use." With that he left.

Sometime later the man called and asked the preacher

to have lunch with him. After lunch he pushed back from the table and said, "Remember what you said to me about my money?" The pastor nodded. "You were right," the man said, bowing his head with embarrassment. "In my present condition I'm of no value to God. About all He could use would be my money."

The next Sunday the man made a public rededication of his life to Christ!

What a tragedy when a man's money is worth more to God than he is. But when one gives himself completely to God, his money is available, just as are his time and his abilities.

Christian availability! Time, talent, money—everything is available when one belongs to the Lord.

Paul, in writing to the Corinthian Christians, told them about the genuine liberality of the churches of Macedonia. Listen to this and examine your own heart. "In a great trial of affliction the abundance of their joy and their deep poverty abounded unto the riches of their liberality. For to their power . . . they were willing of themselves: Praying us with much entreaty that we would receive the gift, and take upon us the fellowship of the ministering to the saints. And this they did, not as we hoped [expected], but first gave their own selves to the Lord and unto us by the will of God" (II Cor. 8:2-5).

Here is Christian availability at its best.

These, I think, are some of the key concepts of Christian stewardship: accountability, dependability, availability. With these concepts stewardship becomes a part of the total Christian response to God and His grace.

## GIVE . . . IN THE SPIRIT OF CHRIST

*II Corinthians 8:9*
*Philippians 2:5-11*

One time during a church financial emphasis a pastor received a written note from a church member complaining that all he ever heard around the church was giving, giving, always giving. "Thanks," wrote the pastor in reply, "for the best definition of Christianity I have ever found: giving, giving, always giving."[1]

When we look for descriptive terms for the life and ministry of Jesus we keep coming back to one term: "He gave." We express it in many ways: "He gave His life a ransom for many." "He gave His life for me." "He gave me healing . . . forgiveness . . . hope . . . new life. . . ." In all the ways we try to describe what Jesus did for us we come back to the fact that He has given.

Little wonder it is, then, that a theme for stewardship emphasis is "Give . . . in the Spirit of Christ."

Two passages of Scripture give ample evidence and breathless statement to the idea of giving in the spirit of Christ. The first passage is found in the context of a plea for giving. In II Corinthians Paul is concerned about the special offering to be given by the Gentile Christians for the aid of the suffering saints in Jerusalem. Paul sought to inspire these Christians to greater giving by the greatest example of all: Jesus Christ. Christ had been rich in heaven. All the wealth of the worlds was His. But for us He gave up everything that could be called wealth. He did it for a purpose: now we could be spiritually rich due to His act of giving.

In Philippians the appeal is to unity and harmony. The people are being asked to lay aside their disharmonies and their discords, to shed their personal ambitions and their pride, their desire for prominence and prestige, and to have in their hearts that humble, selfless desire to serve, which was the very

*25*

essence of the life of Christ. His final and unanswerable appeal for unity is to point at the example of Jesus Christ. In the process we have one of the most exalted and significant statements about Christ.

The familiar words of the King James Version read, "Let this mind be in you, which was also in Christ Jesus. . . ." The *Good News for Modern Man* (Today's English Version) renders it, "The attitude you should have is the one Christ Jesus had. . . ." In this we catch the spirit of our theme: "Give . . . in the spirit of Christ." When we give in the spirit of Christ we catch the attitude of Jesus; we have the mind of the Master. Surely as we think of all that Jesus has given to us and for us, we would be willing to give in the spirit of Christ.

## GIVE IN UNSELFISH LOVE

When we give in the spirit of Christ we will give in unselfish love.

Both of these Scriptural statements point up the unselfishness of the love of Christ for us: He was so unselfish that He renounced the riches of heaven for the poverty of earth; He was so unselfish that He did not grasp His equality with God but He relinquished it to become a wandering teacher of men.

Unselfish love is the highest—and the only legitimate—motive for giving.

Some people give with a selfish motive. They give in order that they might be known as givers, that they might receive some honor, that they be recognized. At heart, this kind of giving is selfish.

Old man Taylor died, over in London, and, in the last moments of his life, began to squirm, as a good many other men do, when they look into eternity. He had never given away any money, but thought he could atone for his miserable life, by giving a thousand pounds to a certain institution in London. When the committee came to fix the matter up, the wretched old miser on his deathbed could not get away from his old habit. He squealed out and asked them if they would not give him 10 percent off for cash. They decided to do it, and he died with a smile on his face, because he had made, or saved, a hundred pounds.[2]

A person giving out of unselfish love does not give for honor or recognition ... does not give for a "cause" ... does not give simply in response to a request.... He gives because of the motive of love and a desire to share.

In Catherine Marshall's novel, *Christy,* Christy Huddleston had gone on a "begging trip" to get funds and equipment for the mountain school. One item received was a piano. At supper the day the piano arrived, Miss Ida, the housekeeper, commented, "Christy Huddleston, you're sure going to get the beggar's reward when you get to heaven."

Others laughed but Miss Alice, the founder and director, did not. She said, "As a matter of fact, Christy, Dr. Ferrand [the director of the mission that had taken over the school] doesn't like begging."

She went on to say:

> "Now's the time to explain the Doctor's philosophy of money and fund-raising," Miss Alice went on, not noticing her at all. "David, you should know this too. He loathes even the term 'raising money.' Whenever he makes a talk about the work—and believe me, that's usually several times a week—he won't even let anyone take a collection afterwards. The point is, Dr. Ferrand won't accept any money unless he knows the individual has had inner direction to give it. He feels that money dunned out of people won't be blessed for the work anyway."

Christy commented to herself:

> These were new ideas to me but I respected them. In fact, in the light of such a philosophy of giving, now I thought I saw what was wrong with the never-ending plea for funds from charitable organizations and pulpits: most of the time these solicitors were trying to pry money out of people by riding roughshod over their individual right of choice.
>
> But Miss Alice continued, "I believe each person has something special he's meant to do. That being the case, surely we have no right to foist 'causes'—even our favorite ones—only present them. Dr. Ferrand believes—and I agree—that only one motive is good enough to warrant

giving: because the self, without pressure, freely chooses to make the gift."[3]

## GIVE IN OBEDIENT SERVICE

Jesus lived in obedience to the will of God. He humbly gave Himself in service to God. His service was to show the love and mercy of God to persons and to give His life in sacrifice for all people. When we give in the spirit of Christ we will give in obedient service.

The focus of Christ was always on people. Our focus must also be on persons. Stewardship is not an abstract term. It is a concrete concept.

Listen to a Sunday school class on Sunday morning.

Thrill to the singing of the choir.

Observe the teaching and training in a Christian training group.

Watch a student go from a Christian college student center to summer missions.

Go down the highway to a remote village and follow the mission pastor as I have into house after house where he spreads the gospel.

Go to a chidren's home and see some boys and girls who have discovered that somebody does really care.

Listen to the testimonies and statements of young people on a youth retreat when they have come to a fresh awareness of the meaning of Christ and faith.

Listen to a lecture in a theological seminary where young servants of the Lord have faith strengthened, minds expanded, and spirits inspired to literally go to the ends of the world with the good news of the gospel.

Watch a homeless, destitute victim of a hurricane light up when he discovers that Christians have given them some clothes to wear and some food to eat. These are the results of stewardship. This is putting Christian stewardship in the concrete.

There may be many things that you cannot do in Christian service. You may not be able to teach. You may not be able to preach. You may not be able to practice medicine in a mission hospital. You may not be able to go as a summer missionary. You may not be able to work in a good will center. You may not be able to help in a rescue mission. But one thing you can do—and can do now—is to give your money in obedient service so that others can render these ministries.

A writer trying to reconstruct the life of the Duke of Wellington said he was helped most by finding an old account book and learning how he spent his money. He thought this was more useful than reading speeches made about the duke or his own public pronouncements. For the way a man spends his money indicates what he thinks is important in life. Giving in obedient service, the Christian can spend his money well.

## GIVE IN WILLING SACRIFICE

The one great thing shown in both these Scriptural messages is the sacrifice of Christ. He gave Himself as a sacrifice. When we give in the spirit of Christ we will give in willing sacrifice.

Now the sacrifice of Christ for us was willingly given. Notice how clearly Paul lets us know that Jesus chose the cross of His own free will. He was not forced to die on the cross: He could have been disobedient to the will of God. He was not driven to the cross: in the Garden of Gethsemane He prayed the prayer of self-surrender that led to the cross. He was not done to death due to circumstances that were beyond His control: He could have acted in ways to placate rather than inflame the religious leaders. No. Jesus gave Himself as a willing sacrifice for us and our sins.

And if we are going to give in the spirit of Christ we will have to give the same way: as a willing sacrifice. We are not asked to give without any regard for what it will cost in terms of money or in terms of things not purchased and not enjoyed. Rather we are asked to give with our eyes wide open. Just as Christ went to the cross with His eyes open, knowing what He was doing, knowing what lay before Him, so are we to give willingly to Christ knowing what it will cost, and knowing what we might have to do without.

But personal sacrifice is not to be considered when we

look at the end results in human lives. Really, most of us have sacrificed very little for the Lord. But if we did, look what it has accomplished. Christ sacrificed His life. But look what it accomplished. It accomplished salvation, the forgiveness of sin, the granting of new life, to all people.

Baptists of the Western Hemisphere were involved in the Crusade of the Americas in 1969. It was an outgrowth of a previous crusade in Brazil. In a meeting for the Brazilian Crusade the question of finances was being discussed. As usual certain discouraging notes were heard.

Finally, Mrs. A. Ben Oliver spoke. She told a story about her parents who were pioneer missionaries to Brazil. A printing press was vital to the work. Timbers supporting the press were giving way with age. The Southern Baptist Foreign Mission Board had no money with which to supply new timbers. Mrs. Oliver's father said, "The printing press must be saved. We must sell our furniture to secure money to purchase the lumber." For months the family sat on boxes and ate their meals from a box used as a table.

Mrs. Oliver concluded by saying that she would sell her furniture, if necessary, in order to finance the cruade. It proved to be unnecessary. But in her heart she had already made the gift. Her reward was to see over 200,000 souls won to Christ.[4]

This is how Christ gave. And we have not actually begun to give until we give in the spirit of Christ.

[1] H. Leo Eddleman, *Teachings of Jesus in Matthew 5:7* (Nashville: Convention Press, 1955), p. 70. Reprinted by permission of the author.

[2] Monroe E. Dodd, *Stewardship Helps for 52 Sundays* (Grand Rapids: Baker Book House, 1958), p. 77. Reprinted by permission of the publisher.

[3] Catherine Marshall, *Christy* (New York: McGraw-Hill Book Co., 1967), pp. 137-138. Used with permission of McGraw-Hill Book Co.

[4] Herschel H. Hobbs, *Studying Life and Work Sunday School Lessons.* April, May, June, 1969 (Nashville: Convention Press, 1969), pp. 33-34. Used by permission.

# THE PURPOSE OF THE TITHE

*Deuteronomy 14:22-29*

When Clare Booth Luce was appointed United States Ambassador to Italy she located a beautiful seventeenth-century Italian villa. She established her residence there. Soon she began to notice a physical deterioration. She was tired. She lost weight. She had little energy. In general her physical condition just got worse and worse.

Of course, she sought medical aid. After a period of intense testing it was found that she was suffering from arsenic poisoning. Every one on her staff was given further security checks. It was soon established that each one could surely be trusted. None of her staff were trying to poison her. Where was the poisoning coming from?

Finally they found the cause. On the ceiling of her bedroom were beautiful designs of roses ornately done in bas relief. It was discovered that they had been painted with a paint that contained arsenic lead. A fine dust fell from these roses. Completely unaware of what was going on Mrs. Luce was being slowly poisoned in her bed by this fine dust falling from the ornate roses on the ceiling.

Completely unaware of it, we are also in danger of being poisoned by the ornate culture and society in which we live. We can be tainted by the materialism that we find around us without ever realizing it. Our attitudes and concepts can be poisoned by the materialistic values of those around us without us ever becoming aware of it until it is too late.

Is there any antidote? Is there anything we can do in a thoroughly materialistic society to help ward off the steady poisoning we receive? One way of counteracting the constant, though possibly unrecognized, poisoning of our values is through Christian giving.

And when we talk about Christians giving we usually talk about tithing. What is its purpose?

Tithing began long before the New Testament. In fact, tithing dates before the Old Testament. The origin of the tithe —giving one-tenth of one's material possessions—is lost in antiquity. Tithing is first mentioned in the Bible in Genesis 14:20, but nothing marks this as the beginning of the custom. Tithing has been found in almost every known country of importance in the ancient world. It was incorporated into the Old Testament law and brought into harmony with the spirit of the law.

The Mosaic Law, interestingly enough, did not limit itself to one tithe, or tenth, but included at least three distinct tithes in addition to an elaborate set of offerings. Classifying the Old Testament tithing structure becomes a difficult job. Robert J. Hastings[1] has summarized it in this manner:

The *first* tithe, known also as the Lord's or the Levite's or the whole tithe, consisted of one-tenth annually, whether of the seed of the land, or of the fruit of the tree, of the herd, or of the flock (Lev. 27:30, 32). This tithe was given for the support of the Levitical priesthood.

The *second* tithe is described in Deuteronomy 12:5-19 and 14:22-27. Three times each year the Hebrews were expected to gather at Jerusalem—for the Passover, for the Feast of Tabernacles, and for the Feast of Weeks. The second tithe paid the travel and expenses of the Hebrews during their stay at Jerusalem. Tithed produce and meat were actually consumed by the worshiper as a part of the ceremony and ritual of the three feasts.

The *third* tithe, given only every three years and kept in the local communities for distribution to the needy (Deut. 14: 28-29 and 26:12-15), was known as a charity tithe.

Counting the two annual tithes, and the third year tithe, the conscientious Hebrew gave 23.33 percent of his income, in addition to the prescribed offerings.

What about the New Testament? Tithing is mentioned only four times in the New Testament. But we realize that the first followers of Christ were strict Jews. Jesus Himself very carefully kept the Law and the ritual. Nowhere was He criticized for not keeping the tithing laws, which He surely would have been had He not done so. There is nothing to indicate that

Christ and the people of the New Testament did not keep and practice and approve tithing.

Where, then, does this put the Christian? The Christian is not legalistically bound to give a tithe. He is morally bound to give out of a heart of love and out of a response to love. Ten percent would be a good place to start. Ten percent, a tithe, has a Biblical precedent. Morally, this would indicate a depth of consecration and sincerity. The Christian's practice of tithing goes beyond tithing itself and involves stewardship—the acknowledgment of our obligation to God and the giving of ourselves and our means to Him. It must grow out of the Christian experience of love, forgiveness, and salvation. It becomes a part of the genuineness of the Christian experience. The tithe is a good starting place with a strong Biblical precedent for Christian giving.

Keeping this in mind, notice the purpose of the tithe as we find it in Deuteronomy 14.

## AN ACT OF REMEMBRANCE

The purpose of the tithe is an act of remembrance. A tenth of the agricultural products and the firstlings of the herds and flocks were to be taken to the central sanctuary. If it was too far to travel, they could be sold and the money taken there.

This was to remind the people that the land is God's and that all good things come from His hands. When the late Bishop Edwin H. Hughes (Methodist) was a young pastor he served a rural parish in the Middle West. One day in preaching he said that we own nothing: it all belongs to God.

Following the service a farmer took the minister home for dinner, and after a sumptuous meal the two men walked out to see the broad acres of farm land, with all that was on them. The farmer told how his wife and he had started out without a dime from anyone else, and worked for all they had. "If we don't own this farm, who does?" was the farmer's question to the preacher.

The young minister replied in a kind tone of voice, "Will you ask me that question one hundred years from today?"

Every time we give this should serve as a reminder to us.

Notice that these portions of the tithe were to be eaten at the central sanctuary in an act of worship. The purpose of the tithe is found in an act of worship.

When we give our money to God it is as an act of worship.

This is one way that we give ourselves to God. When I was a junior in high school someone once mentioned that we should figure how much work it cost at the hourly rate we received for our work to go to a movie or to buy a milk shake or to do whatever we might do that costs money. This impressed me somewhat as I was making my living at that time by selling ladies' shoes on Saturdays. I began to do it. For everything I spent I computed its cost in terms of minutes or hours worked. One thing that it will surely do: it will make you more careful about how you spend your money. Another thing it will do is show that we give ourselves—or spend ourselves—in the way we use time. When we worship we are turning a part of ourselves to God.

In this act of worship through giving we are taking part of the responsibility upon ourselves for doing God's work.

Porter Routh, executive secretary of the Executive Committee of the Southern Baptist Convention, once showed this in an article he wrote.

He said: George Mason was one of the great laymen I knew as a boy. Mr. Mason was one of those men who seemed to be talking with the Lord in very personal, intimate terms when he was called on for prayer.

In Cliff Temple, Dallas, where I grew up, we would remember the needs of the fellowship in prayer on Wednesday night. Dr. Wallace Bassett would often call on George Mason, big heart and all, to remember the particulars of problems brought to light.

On one Wednesday night, Mr. Mason mentioned one man who had been in a hospital for a long time. He was going home the next day to a family faced with desperate financial problems. Mr. Mason prayed that the Lord would put it on the heart of some member to take some groceries to the house.

He went on to mention several other subjects, and then he suddenly interrupted himself by praying:

"Now, Lord! about those groceries I mentioned earlier. Don't worry about that. I am taking care of them myself."

This is one of our real problems in stewardship. We forget we have a personal responsibility. We are like the man who kept driving around the courthouse square looking for some unused time on the parking meter so he could "park on some other man's nickel."

## AN ACT OF MERCY

The purpose of the tithe is found in an act of mercy. Did you notice that in the Deuteronomy passage one of the uses of the tithe was for acts of mercy for the poor and the landless? These were the people who could not care for themselves. Through the tithe they were given provision.

Our tithing today does the very same thing. We are able to provide help where help is needed, both spiritually and physically. The total program of the church is designed to give some substance to Christian concern in action.

When we realize that we are people who are the recipients of God's mercy trying to show mercy to others then we get stewardship into something of the right perspective.

I heard Grady Wilson, associate of Billy Graham, tell of a trip to a leper colony in Nigeria while on crusades in Africa. Billy Graham preached in a special service. During the service an offering was taken and the sum of two pounds (about $5.00) was collected. When the collection was given to him he was also given the assurance that these people were always interested in his work and concerned about his crusades and prayerful about their success. As they left the colony Graham said to Wilson and Cliff Barrows, "Fellows, that's the secret. That's the secret of the success of our team."

And that's the secret of Christian stewardship, too. We have all received God's mercy. When we tithe we recognize this mercy from God and seek to show it to others.

What you give to God and His work will be determined

by your own heart and experience. Tithing is a place to start. It has Biblical precedent and it has good purposes.

[1] Robert J. Hastings, *My Money and God* (Nashville: Broadman Press, 1961), p. 62. Reprinted by permission of the author.

# PRINCIPLES OF CHRISTIAN GIVING

## II Corinthians 8:1-15

"All the world loves a lover," it is said. It is also true that all the world loves a giver. Think of the number of people who have been set before us as great examples of Christian love and grace, chiefly for one reason: the fact that they would give of their material means to others.

How many times have we heard of the example of R. G. LeTourneau who has turned the profits of his business into missions and benevolent enterprises in other countries, or of William Fleming who, during his lifetime, gave thousands of dollars at a time to Southern Baptist educational institutions and to mission causes, or of Maxie Jarmen who built a string of church houses throughout South America? And we have forgotten the very strong feelings many of our grandparents or great grandparents had for such people as Andrew Carnegie, John D. Rockefeller, and Henry Ford. When we think of those men today we usually think in terms of the Carnegie libraries, the Rockefeller Foundation or the Ford Foundation which have financed scientific and educational research that probably could never have been done otherwise. But the fact that these men left fortunes to be *given* obscures other facts about them. And the same is true for some Texans who have been our contemporaries, such as Sid Richardson and Hugh Roy Collum. We have honored these people because they have given much.

But, of course, there is the usual reply, "Why shouldn't they give, they had it to give." What I want us to think about now goes beyond just giving. And it goes beyond discussing those who are able to give. I want us to consider some principles for Christian giving. If we are asked to give, there must be reasons or principles behind it. That's what I want us to try to uncover: some principles for Christian giving.

A good place to look for these principles is in II Corinthians 8 and 9. Paul is talking about a special offering here. The Christians in Jerusalem were in dire need. And Paul called upon the Gentile Christians to help them by taking up a special collection. We see some mention of it in I Corinthians. And here in II Corinthians considerable space is taken up with the subject of this special offering for the Jewish brothers in want. Now there were good reasons for Paul to want this offering to be a success. For one thing, it would do great things for Christian brotherhood. Some of the Jerusalem Christians had been a little hesitant about taking the gospel to the Gentiles. Even though they had been told to be witnesses in Jerusalem, Judea, and Samaria they had hugged Jerusalem until persecution drove them out. And as they went, they preached. This would be an act of generosity to help show the brotherhood between the Jewish Christians and the Gentile Christians. But it would also be the basic Christian response of love to another's need. Paul could come back with visible proof of the work of grace in the hearts of these Gentiles.

In making this appeal to the Corinthians, he sets out what I want to call "principles of Christian giving." We can see in these verses some of the principles upon which we base our giving.

## A THEOLOGICAL PRINCIPLE: GRACE

Now don't let the terminology—"theological principle"—scare you. By theology I have reference here to a basic belief about God. And that basic belief about God can be expounded in one word: grace. No matter how much or how little formal theology we know, we are all acquainted with one thing: and that one thing is that we are saved by the grace of God, that we are preserved by the grace of God, that our very existence depends on the grace of God.

Grace is basic in Paul's appeal to these people. And grace is basic to my appeal to you. Grace is basic in the matter of our giving of material possessions to God and His work. The whole activity that Paul has reference to in this passage of Scripture is described by the repeated use of the word *grace*. It occurs seven times in the eighth chapter and three times in chapter nine. The whole subject of giving, of the collection for the saints, is looked upon throughout this section as an activity of grace. Notice how the section begins in 8:1. He is telling them about the grace of God on the Macedonian churches. And what did the Macedonian churches do? Why they gave exceedingly well to this collection for the saints.

Grace is seen, first, in God's ownership of all things. It is plain fact that the Bible teaches that God is the ultimate owner of all things. Listen to the psalmist. "The earth is the Lord's, and the fulness thereof, the world, and they that dwell therein." (Ps. 24:1). "For every beast of the forest is mine, and the cattle upon a thousand hills" (Ps. 50:10). And there was a chorus we used to sing that said:

> He owns the cattle on a thousand hills,
>     The wealth of every mine.
> He owns the rivers, and the rocks, and rills,
>     The sun and moon that shine.

All of which points up the very first thing we know about God's grace. And that is that it is entirely by the grace of God that we enjoy any of the comforts of the earth and the riches of the earth.

But grace also serves as an example for us. "For ye know the grace of our Lord Jesus Christ, that, though he was rich, yet for your sakes he became poor, that ye through his poverty might be rich" (vs. 9). Whenever we think about giving and grace we quickly understand that we can't outgive the grace of God. God has shown us His grace in allowing us to use and enjoy His possessions. But God has even more shown us grace in that Christ gave up willingly the riches of heaven to become man—by grace. And this was done for the reason of our salvation. By His grace we became redeemed. By His poverty we became rich. For this grace we ought to be grateful.

And this brings out the third thing we see about grace in giving. Giving itself is a grace. Notice that in verse 7 he tells them of other things that they abound in, and "this grace also." And what is this grace? Giving. So this puts Christian giving on a very high plane. As we are to abound in faith, eloquence, knowledge, enthusiastic zeal, and love, so are we also to abound in the grace of giving. This needs cultivating just as do the other Christian graces.

And so grace is a theological principle in giving, a principle based on our basic beliefs about God. God is owner of all things and bestows these things on us by His grace. His grace has provided us with salvation, and then grace prompts us to give in a Christian, Christlike spirit. Even as Christ gave for us: willingly, lovingly, not mechanically, are we to give for Him: with a willing heart, a loving spirit, and a generosity that doesn't look for a legal stopping place.

## A HUMAN PRINCIPLE: SHARING

The first principle was based on the nature of God: grace. Now let us look at a principle that finds its basis in the human heart: the desire to share what we have with others.

The first thing that I think we should note about sharing is that it is not based on a superfluity of goods. You don't share just because you have a lot and can afford it. Go back to verses 2 and 3. These were people who had suffered and were in affliction. As J. B. Phillips translates it they were down to their last penny. But they were willing to give to the limits of their means and beyond their means, to share with others.

This is the very heart of Christian concern. People give of their money to the church and to the work of the Lord—not because they have so much that they wouldn't miss it—but because of a deep desire to share what they have with others. If you wait until you can afford to tithe you will never do it. The time to start is right now. It may seem that you can't live without it, but somehow you do.

I remember well the testimony of Alvin Dark, of baseball fame, when he sent the tithe of his World Series money when he was a player with the New York Giants to his home church. It was a check for over a thousand dollars sent to the Trinity Baptist Church in Lake Charles, Louisiana. When it made headlines across the country he couldn't quite understand it. He said, "Why, I began tithing when I made $3.00 a week on a newspaper route." And this is where Christian giving starts.

Not with great sums of money. But with small sums, even if it means giving beyond the limits of your means.

But there is another human element that shows up in sharing through Christian giving. That is the fellowship of sharing. Notice that verse 4 says that these Macedonians urged the gift upon Paul so that they could have part in "the fellowship of the ministering to the saints." What a wonderful way that is to express the reality of Christian giving. When you give your money to the church and to the service of the Lord you have then become a part of the fellowship of sharing.

Think of the many great ways that this fellowship expresses itself. You are a part of the preaching of the gospel and of the singing of the praises of God. You have a fellowship in providing this place to worship. And also in building houses of worship around the world. You have a fellowship of sharing in the healing of the sick and the caring for old folks, and the keeping of orphans. Through Christian giving we are able to take part in a great fellowship of sharing that we could not do in any other way. Once Porter Routh, secretary-treasurer of the Executive Committee of the Southern Baptist Convention, said with reference to the Southern Baptist Convention Co-Operative Program for world missions:

> Last summer I saw young men being trained in a seminary in Zurich, Switzerland. I saw children in an orphanage in Rome, Italy. I saw victims of leprosy being treated in Nigeria. All of these services were made possible through the Co-Operative Program. The Co-Operative Program is in the heart of a farmer in Arkansas, a housewife in Mississippi, a mill worker in North Carolina, an oilfield worker in Texas. The Co-Operative Program is within your own heart as you use its services to share Christ with the whole world.

This is a very human element or principle in our Christian giving: a desire to share what we have with others. This is a sharing in giving that begins now, where we are, with a little rather than waiting in hopes of having a lot sometime. This sharing creates a great fellowship of sharing which gives us a warmth of knowing that we are a part of a great act of mercy and service of God.

I never fail to read verse 5 without getting a certain thrill out of it. "And this they did, not as we hoped, but first gave their own selves to the Lord, and unto us by the will of God." ". . . first gave their own selves to the Lord . . . ," this is the beginning of all Christian stewardship. It begins with giving yourself to the Lord. You never begin to give to God until you have given yourself to God. Oh, you might tip God a bit. You might make a handout to Him at times. But you have not really given until first you place yourself in His service and at His disposal.

I discovered something recently that I had overlooked in the reading of a very familiar passage of Scripture: Romans 10:9-10. In the King James Version it says, "That if thou shalt confess with thy mouth the Lord Jesus, and shalt believe in thine heart that God hath raised him from the dead, thou shalt be saved. For with the heart man believeth unto righteousness; and with the mouth confession is made unto salvation." Now the discovery was in the way the American Standard Version translates that. It says "If thou shalt confess with thy mouth Jesus as Lord [or as the marginal translation has it "Jesus is Lord"], and shalt believe in thy heart that God raised him from the dead, thou shalt be saved. . . ." This is the earliest confession of the church, "Jesus is Lord." And what Paul has said is that if you believe that Jesus is the Son of God, that God raised Him from the dead, and you are willing to make it the confession of your life then salvation comes to you. No one is ever saved except in the atmosphere of a surrender to Christ as Lord, Lord of heaven, Lord of earth, Lord of me, and Lord of mine. That is what the phrase "Jesus is Lord" means. And as I come into this relationship with Christ, this becomes the confession that characterizes the relationship.

Now this is what I am saying about dedication. Our dedication as Christians must be to this fact that Christ is really Lord of all. If Christ is Lord of all then He is Lord also of all that I have. Growing out of this relationship of servant and Lord is Christian stewardship. This relationship where I am slave and Jesus is Master, where I am owned and God is the owner is the relationship that begins all of Christian stewardship.

But the basic problem is that many have not made that beginning promise yet. To dedicate yourself to God, to really acknowledge the Lordship of Christ is to make Christ Lord of every area and every facet of life. If we do not see ourselves as owned by Jesus Christ, then there will never be New Testament stewardship. And I think of those verses in I Corinthians 6:19-20: "What? Know ye not that your body is the temple of the Holy Ghost which is in you, which ye have of God, and ye are not your own? For ye are bought with a price. . . ."

Let me tell you of two people in Fort Worth to whom this is a reality. Their story has been related by Kenneth Chafin. They live in one of these shell houses. When they bought it, it was just a shell with plumbing, and that was it. With their hands and with sheetrock you can haul home in the back of a car, and with skill you can get with bedding and taping and extra time, they finished the inside of that house. He worked down at Stripling's. He does not make $200 per month, and they never had a more faithful employee than that man. The children are grown. She works in the mail order department of Montgomery Ward. Combined, I doubt seriously if they make $350 a month. Their pastor knew that they were tithing people, but was not ready for them to do what they did when it came to the mission offering. They came with an enormous amount of money, and when asked where they got it, they said, "We have saved our change. All the dimes we get in our change we save for 365 days so that we can have a worthy offering when we give to our mission offering." When they gave their tithing testimony this is what they said, "We tithe because not only did God make us, but when we were sinners He loved us and died for us, and Mr. O'Neill came down and told us of that love, and we believed and were born again. Our lives have been different, and we belong to Him, and everything that we have belongs to Him." This is dedication to God. This is Christian stewardship.

Why do we give to God and the church? These are the reasons. And basic is the response of love to Christ our Lord.

# LESSONS FROM LIFE ABOUT STEWARDSHIP

*Luke 16:1-13*

Many years ago I read an autobiography of the late Bernard Baruch, the famous financier and adviser to presidents. In this autobiography he said that in his early days of stock speculation in which he amassed his initial fortune, whenever he had completed any deal he would take a few days off and think about and analyze what he had done. Whether he made money or lost money he would try to reconstruct all that he had done step by step in an effort to learn all that he could from that transaction. He was learning a lesson from life.

In the Bible we learn many lessons from life about many things. In fact, it is sometimes quite shocking to see some of the figures that Jesus used to bring us to a point of revelation about ourselves or about God. All His figures are not haloed saints. To be sure He used a sovereign freedom in His choice of characters for His parables. Think of some of them that might seem to be rather unlikely prospects for a religious lesson: the prodigal son, who pictured selfishness and dissipation; the elder brother of the prodigal son, who pictured sullen obedience and self-righteousness; the hardhearted judge, who was not moved by justice or pity to grant the widow's request but acted simply to quiet her incessant pleas. And in this parable we have what William Barclay calls "about as choice a set of rascals as one could meet anywhere."[1]

The central character, the unjust steward, is a rascal. When he was let out of his job he immediately knew that he would have to do something. He had no inclination to work physically. He was too proud to beg. So he decided on fraud. The debtors were also rascals. They seemingly had no compunction about changing their bills to show that they did not owe the landowner as much as they really did. The master himself was a rascal. Evidently he just dismissed the steward, who was the administrator of his estate, without any hearing or examination of the justice of the charges that had been made against him. But then when he learned of the steward's shrewd actions, he commended him for his foxy behavior, although there is no evidence that he gave him his job back. From this "choice set of rascals" it seems unusual that we could get any real meaningful spiritual teaching. But indeed we do. This is a lesson from life about stewardship.

The immediate context of this parable goes back to the fifteenth chapter. There, Jesus had told the three interrelated parables of the lost coin, the lost sheep, and the lost boy to justify His actions before the Pharisees, to show that He was really displaying the heart of God in receiving and eating with sinners. Then immediately on the heels of this He told three other parables. Two of them, the first and third, were addressed to His disciples. The middle one, the parable of the rich man and Lazarus, was addressed to the Pharisees and Sadducees to show them the immutability of the decisions that we make on this earth. This parable was directed to the disciples but was told in the presence of the critics of the Master.

Jesus took a picture from everyday life, that of the foreman (or administrator or overseer) defrauding the landowner and drew from it some very valuable lessons from life about stewardship. Usually a parable has only one main point, one central teaching. But this one is different. In the Scripture itself, we have several important lessons drawn. These are indeed lessons from life about stewardship.

## PRUDENCE

The first lesson that is drawn in the Scripture is that which is found in verse 8. "And the Lord [the lord of the servant not Jesus the Lord] commended the unjust steward, because he had done wisely [for his prudence, RSV]." To this Jesus added, "for the children of this world are in their generation wiser than the children of light."

Now you will notice that the steward is not commended for his morality nor for his honesty, but simply for his prudence. By reducing the bills of the debtors he had indebted them to him.

He had provided for himself some friends for his use when he was out of work. He had made them accomplices in his dishonesty. And, if worse came to worse, he was in a fine position for a little judicious blackmail. Now, no judgment is passed on the morality of what the man had done—it is clearly and admittedly an immoral and dishonest thing. But he did use a bit of shrewd foresight in taking care of himself, even if it was dishonest. And it is at this point that Jesus applied the lesson.

Could you even imagine what kind of powerful Christians we would be and what kind of a witnessing church we would have if Christians used the same kind of resourcefulness in their spiritual life as they do in their business life? Businessmen slave day and night to make their pile of money. Ardent communists, though they have no hope of a hereafter, devote all their time and talents to spreading their propaganda and collaring key positions. All of us take all kinds of precaution by way of insurance and bonds and social security against the chances and changes of this world, while we neglect to do anything to prepare ourselves for the next one. If we were as prudent in our efforts at our spiritual life as we are in things of the world, what could we not do!

If we were as prudent in abandoning ourselves and being unconcerned about what others think of us in our spiritual life and work as we are in the things of the world, what could we not do for Christ! We are all awfully afraid of the charge of fanaticism. The person who will not knock on doors to visit for the church will go house to house selling cakes for his civic club at Christmastime. The person who will not say amen or allow a tear to fall in a worship service lest someone think him emotional does not hold back any emotion in a Shriner's parade. The person who will not get involved in the work of the church through a committee assignment or a Sunday school class office will take on any assignment given him in any other organization to which he belongs and will carry it out with interest and enthusiasm. We hardly think people will call us fanatics for the PTA or Lion's Club or Rotary or the Masonic Order. But the merest suggestion of it in religion sends shudders up and down our backs and keeps us from effective service.

And what should I say about the amount of money spent on these things? I know how much it costs to belong to a service club and a garden club. Because I do a little of it I know how much it costs to hunt and to fish and to golf and to bowl. Hobbies are expensive whether it is woodworking or doll collecting. Can we really call ourselves good stewards, good managers of the things God has entrusted to us, when we spend more effort, more interest, more time, and more money on the things of this life and this world than we do on spiritual things? This is the first lesson from life about stewardship. It is a lesson about prudence.

## USEFULNESS

The second lesson that is drawn in this parable is about the use of money. In verse 9 we are admonished to use money, the material possessions that we have (that is the meaning of mammon), to make friends for ourselves in eternity. Now this is exactly what the unjust steward did. He used money to make friends for himself in this world. He made sure that he had a place to go when he was turned out of his job. If a crass materialist like this could find the usefulness in money, couldn't a person with a spiritual bent, a Christian, do much more with it? Why he could use it, make friends for himself for all eternity! It cannot be used to buy our way into heaven or to buy off God because of our sin or to ease a guilty conscience. But it can be used to purchase things and to do things the value of which lasts throughout eternity. Who can begin to estimate the eternal value of the amount of money necessary to provide a room, a chair, light and heat, and a Sunday school quarterly for one Beginner child? This money will be used to make for ourselves friends in eternal habitations.

Helmut Thielicke, in speaking of the unjust steward, points out the following:

> . . . this man used money and possessions *for* something, they were not an end in themselves. If a purely material-istic child of the world like the dishonest steward can man-age on *his* level to compel money to serve his ends and thus give it its relative importance, how much more—and at the same time, how differently—should the children of

light do this on their level! . . . he is above his money and not a slave to it. He compels the money to perform a service. The money will one day forsake him, but those whom he has helped with it will remain faithful to him and take him in.[2]

The late G. A. Studdert-Kennedy once said that the real meaning of money was brought home to him when he saw a girl dying of tuberculosis while she lived "in one of those abominable pigsties which do duty for houses for a considerable portion of our population." The girl *could* get well, but only on one condition: somebody had to find enough money to transport her to a decent place where she could have fresh air, professional care, and good food. Studdert-Kennedy went out and got the money and then he knew, he said, what money is. "It is the power to demand a human service and to be sure that you will get it."[3]

And this is exactly what Jesus had reference to here. Think of the human services for the cause of Christ that we can demand if we have the money to be sure that we get it: literature, hospitals, places of worship, adequate staffs, the gospel carried to the world.

So another lesson from life that we learn about stewardship has to do with the usefulness of money—that we will not make it an idol, or a god, but a servant, something to be used in the service of God for the good of mankind.

## FAITHFULNESS

In verses 10 through 12 Jesus draws another lesson for us. In addition to lessons about prudence and usefulness he points out the matter of faithfulness. If we have not been faithful in such a small matter as the stewardship of our material possessions, how can we expect to be entrusted with the true riches, spiritual riches? If we have not been faithful to God with that money which incidentally passes through our hands, how can we expect to be faithful to Him with that which is our own, our very lives?

Ralph A. Herring says that this text "seems to be saying that tithing is the ABC's of stewardship. Faithfulness at this point is rewarded by the privilege of handling life's true riches and ultimately coming into possession of them forever."

He went on to say:

An experience in my first pastorate at Crestwood, Kentucky, confirms this observation. Walking one day past a big garage in Louisville, a shrill whistle attracted my attention to an open window on the floor above. I recognized instantly the grimy face of a mechanic who had moved a few months before from Crestwood into the big city. His first name was Earl. He motioned me to come up, explaining with a grin, "You don't have to punch the clock, but I would if I came down to you!"

His first question was, "Are there night classes at the seminary where a man like me could go deeper in Bible study?" My face must have registered utter astonishment for he broke into a laugh upon seeing my reaction.

The truth is he was about the last man on earth from whom I would have expected such an inquiry. I knew him only as one of those Baptists who would come to church but could never be prevailed upon to move his membership!

But one can never anticipate the effect of God's word. Unknown to me a sermon on tithing had found its mark. Earl would not have recognized his account of what followed that sermon as a witness to tithing. That is what made it so effective. He and his wife had resolved to tithe as a result of that sermon. Very soon afterwards a better job at fifty dollars per week opened up in the city.

"I told my wife," he said, "that if we were going to tithe we'd have to take it to the church, and on the following Sunday I dropped five dollars into the plate. One of the ushers saw it and afterwards made us feel very welcome," he added with a smile. "Then we figured if we were going to put our money into the church we might as well join, so we did."

He had become a teacher of a Sunday school class of boys. "I love it," he said, "but I must know my Bible better. That is why I am asking you about night studies at the seminary."

. . . He showed me that tithing is really the ABC's of stewardship. He had become faithful in that which is least and God was promoting him to the "true riches" of his manifold grace.[4]

## MASTERY

In verse 13 we have a verse that also appears in the Sermon

on the Mount. Jesus was saying that we cannot at the same time serve God as God and mammon, or material possessions, as a god. This is the rule that no slave can serve two masters. Slavery was very common in the days of Jesus. One fact about slavery was that the master possessed the slave and possessed him exclusively. People today can do a certain amount of "moonlighting." They can work for someone during the day and also work for someone else at night or on weekends or in their off hours. This was not possible in slavery. The master of the slave was his master exclusively. And this is just what Jesus is getting at about our relationship with God. When we accept Christ and make Him Lord of our lives then He is to be the Lord exclusively. And God is a jealous God. He will not share our allegiance with anything so inanimate as money.

Martin Luther once said that every man needed two conversions, "one of the heart and another of the pocketbook." I hate to differ with such a figure as Martin Luther; but at this point he is dead wrong! Every man needs one conversion—a conversion that makes him a child of God, a servant of Jesus Christ, a subject of the Lord God—and that conversion must include not only his heart but every part of his being and life, including his pocketbook.

This is the very point at which Christian stewardship must begin. This is the most important lesson from life about stewardship. Stewardship doesn't begin with obligation. Stewardship doesn't begin with legality. Stewardship doesn't begin with fear. Stewardship doesn't begin with desire for gain. Stewardship begins with mastery . . . the making of Christ Lord and master of our lives.

When we understand the exclusiveness of salvation, how that accepting Christ as Savior and master excludes all else, then we see that it all falls into place. If Christ is indeed master of our lives then we will be prudent and wise in our efforts and energy; then we will see that our material possessions are not ours to worship but to use, and to use in such a way that they can be used for God's glory throughout eternity; then we will be faithful in the small things that God has entrusted to us, like handling money, and in proving our faithfulness He will entrust greater things to our care, like leading men. But it all begins with mastery —Jesus Christ must be the absolute master of our lives.

Life teaches us many lessons. One lesson that it teaches us is our need of salvation and forgiveness of sin. But it also teaches us that in accepting Christ as Savior we also accept Him as Lord and Master. If He is Master He must be exclusively the Master of our lives—and a part of life is our stewardship, our administration of the things entrusted to our care. These are lessons from life about stewardship. And they begin with the acceptance of Christ, making Him Master of your life.

[1] From *The Gospel of Luke,* translated and interpreted by William Barclay. Published in the U.S.A. by The Westminster Press, 1957. p. 215. Used by permission.

[2] Helmut Thielicke, *The Waiting Father,* trans. John W. Doberstein (New York: Harper and Brothers, 1959), p. 101. Reprinted by permission of the publisher.

[3] Cited in Elton Trueblood, *Foundations for Reconstruction* (New York: Harper and Brothers, 1946), p. 81. Reprinted by permission of the publisher.

[4] Ralph A. Herring, "The ABC's of Stewardship," *The Baptist Program* (July, 1965), pp. 4-5. Reprinted by permission of the publisher.

## WHAT TITHING WILL NOT DO

*Matthew 23:23*

One of the things that triggered the Protestant Reformation led by Martin Luther in the sixteenth century was an attitude expressed toward money.

The practice of granting indulgences arose in the Roman Catholic Church during the Crusades. The theory was that the saints had provided a treasury of merits by their good deeds. For a price, others could draw from this treasury of merits. At first indulgences were granted only to those who had sacrificed or risked their lives in fighting the infidel. Then they were extended to those who could not go, but made contributions to the enterprise. Later they were extended to cover the construction of churches, monasteries, and hospitals. The gothic cathedrals were financed in this way.

Luther had several times spoken out against the indulgences. But the thing that brought on Luther's severe reaction against them was the process used in selling indulgences for the construction of St. Peter's Basilica in Rome. One of those who sold them was a Dominican monk named John Tetzel. He was not allowed to go into electoral Saxony where Luther ministered but he did go just to the border and some of the people from Saxony went across and bought the indulgences.

In selling them he had a little rhyme he quoted:

> As soon as the coin in the coffer rings,
> The soul from purgatory springs.

This infuriated Luther. On the Eve of All Saints' Day (Halloween) in 1517 Luther nailed his Ninety-Five Theses or propositions for debate on the door of the Castle Church in Wittenberg. Luther knew that there were some things money could not do.

And perhaps we need to be reminded of this occasionally ourselves. Especially during the time of stewardship emphases we might give so much attention to the beneficent results of Christian giving that we give the idea that this is the sum of Christianity. Tithing, especially, is presented sometimes in such a way that it might seem that it is the apex of Christian life.

There are many things that tithing will do. It will acknowledge God's ownership of all things. It will follow a solid Biblical precedent in the amount of money to give. It will give a sense of partnership, of involvement, of obedience. It will bring spiritual blessings. Tithing will do these things. But there are some things that tithing will not do.

Jesus recognized this Himself. In one of the four references to tithing in the New Testament Jesus commended the Pharisees for their scrupulous attention given to the tithe. But at the same time He criticized them heavily for leaving undone some of the important things in the life of a godly person. Jesus was not criticizing the tithe. He was criticizing the substitution of the tithe for justice, mercy, and faith.

These words are found in a section of Matthew 23 that contains seven woes on the Pharisees. In seven particulars Jesus accuses them of missing the real spirit of spiritual life. Now the Jews were commanded to tithe. And the Pharisees did tithe. But they carried it to the extreme of even computing the tenth of the kitchen herbs grown in the flower bed. That would be all right if they had gone on to add positive character to their life. But that is where they stopped. Jesus' comment to them was that tithing they ought to have done, but not to have left the other undone.

This suggests some things tithing will not do.

## TITHING WILL NOT PUT YOU
## IN A POSITION TO BARGAIN WITH GOD

Some people understand the matter of stewardship as making a bargain with God—that God is obligated to them because they give to Him. It is thought of as an attempt to win the favor of God, something that is done to earn His favor and reward.

This is not a new thing. It was done as long ago as the Old Testament times. Jacob did it:

> And Jacob vowed a vow, saying, If God will be with
> me, and will keep me in this way that I go, and will give
> me bread to eat, and raiment to put on,
>
> So that I come again to my father's house in peace;
> then shall the Lord be my God:
>
> And this stone, which I have set for a pillar, shall be
> God's house: and of all that thou shalt give me I will
> surely give the tenth unto thee. —Genesis 28:20-22

When this attitude is followed several things can result.

One can think that God is obligated to keep him from harm, disaster, tragedy. God has never promised that being a Christian, to say nothing of giving as a Christian, will automatically protect us from any harm or disaster. After all, Jesus went to the cross.

I know a Baptist deacon who was very disappointed in his children. Even though he had little formal education he desired very strongly that his children would get a good education. But only one of seven had graduated from high school at that time. There had been some scrapes and difficulties. Now one daughter was about to give birth to an illegitimate baby. When I ran into him one day in another town he was full of bitterness. "Why did God let this happen to me?" he questioned. "Ever since I have been a Christian I have taught Sunday school, I have been a deacon, and I have tithed. Why would God let me suffer like this?" Probably without realizing it he was assuming that God was obligated to him. But He was not.

Or sometimes it is interpreted in a more materialistic way: that God is obligated to increase the wealth of one who tithes, that God rewards the faithful giver.

Does it pay to tithe? Robert J. Hastings answers this question well:

> Yes, it does "pay" to tithe, if by payment one means
> a satisfied conscience, a joy in knowing one's dollars are
> at work day and night winning men to Christ; or if one
> means a keener appreciation for and better management
> of money or God's privilege to bestow material blessings,
> if and when he chooses.
>
> No, a thousand times no, it does not pay to tithe if
> one means "insurance" against all known catastrophes, an
> increase in income for every step-up in giving, fewer doctor

bills and immunity from accidents. This "No" is sounded from the ash heap where sits Job scraping his boils with a potsherd, a man whose only fault that Satan could find was his faith in God. This "No" echoes from Calvary where writhes in agony One who gave not a tenth but all that he had, and whose only reward was the spittle of his jeerers and the piercing nails of his executioners.

This is not said to deny the validity of unnumbered testimonies of conscientious tithers whose cups have been filled to overflowing in their practice of Christian stewardship. It is said to warn against the promise of material rewards as a motive for giving, and to resay that sometimes adversity is a reward and bitterness a blessing.[1]

Samuel E. Maddox, son of missionary parents, tells an experience that beautifully expresses the Christian position on rewards.

His parents, Mr. and Mrs. O. P. Maddox, had just returned to Rio de Janeiro in 1914 from furlough. The customs officials, thinking they were wealthy American business people, pronounced such high import duties that the missionaries were unable to claim their luggage. Little did these officials dream that the annual salary of this couple was a mere four hundred dollars, plus travel and housing.

Some time later Mrs. Maddox was bathing their one-year-old son. She left him a few moments to answer the door. When she returned, the child had drowned. In an effort to revive the lifeless form, four doctors worked unsuccessfully for two hours.

Following the burial, as they were getting into the carriage for the return trip into the city, Mrs. Maddox said, "What is this strange joy that I feel in my heart on this darkest day of our lives?" Mr. Maddox replied, "This is Christ's promise to be with us to the end of the age!"

The next day's mail brought exorbitant bills from the four doctors (who also thought they were wealthy) and their small salary check. For the first time in his life, Mr. Maddox wondered whether it would be right to withhold some of their tithe. Mrs. Maddox spoke up, "No, let us give as we always have. Even if we used our tithe, it would not begin to meet our obligations."

To make a long story short, friends intervened, the doctor bills were greatly reduced, and the customs removed. But the greatest victory was not in God's providence in helping meet their bills—it was the faith He gave this missionary couple to say, "God is first in our lives."

Their son, Dr. Samuel Maddox, in commenting on this experience says, "When father and mother died, they had very little of this world's goods, but they left me with a priceless heritage, a memory of parents who dared to put God first in all of life's experiences."[2]

We cannot say, then, conscientiously that tithing will put us in a positon to bargain with God.

## TITHING WILL NOT SUBSTITUTE
## FOR GENUINE CHRISTIAN CHARACTER

This is the point that Jesus was making. The people in question were tithing, all right. They were scrupulously, minutely, exactingly tithing. But they were not doing much with the development of a Godlike character.

We cannot allow the attitude that we show toward giving overshadow the attitude that we have toward developing genuine Christian character and helping our fellowmen in love.

Justice, mercy, and faith are all absolute essentials in living the Christian life.

Money, alone, will not bring happiness.

"Silver Threads Among the Gold" was written around the turn of the century by Hart P. Danks in tribute to a happy home and family. The song was an unexpected hit, and the royalties poured in. But there was disagreement over how to spend the new-found wealth. Separation followed. Danks died alone in a rooming house in Philadelphia. Nearby was found an old copy of the song with these words written across it, "It's hard to grow old alone."[3]

Even giving money, alone, will not bring happiness. But giving your money, acknowledging your stewardship and accountability to God, *and* practicing justice, mercy, and faith will bring happiness and contentment and fullness to life.

Judgment is the deep concern for justice in the world; mercy is a love of compassion toward the weakest and worst;

faith is fidelity to righteousness and mercy in daily life. When these things are practiced the sincerity of Christian commitment can be seen.

## TITHING WILL NOT TAKE
## THE PLACE OF A COMMITMENT OF LIFE
## TO GOD AND HIS WILL

You cannot escape the demand of the commitment of your life to Christ simply by the practice of tithing. Sometimes people seem to think that if they give some of their money to God that is all that is necessary. But it is not. The whole matter of Christian faith must begin with the commitment of life in faith and trust to Christ as Savior.

If you begin with the commitment of life to Christ then you will be willing to follow Him in whatever direction this leads. This will include giving, even tithing . . . the struggle to develop Christian character and attitudes . . . witnessing . . . following God in vocation or simply in opportunities that are available for Christian service. Sometimes this may mean making a decision, deciding between attractive alternatives. But we must be open to God's leadership. We cannot be unless we are first committed to Him and His will.

George Beverly Shea is known around the world as the soloist in Billy Graham's evangelistic crusades. In his autobiography *Then Sings My Soul* he tells of the turning point in his life in a chapter entitled "The Big Break I Didn't Take." When he was twenty-seven years of age he was working as a medical secretary for the Mutual Life Insurance Company in New York City. At other times he exercised his greatest love—singing. He was then making $34.50 per week.

He received an opportunity to audition for the Lynn Murray Singers, a group he described as "the Fred Waring group of that day." While waiting for the audition he learned that in addition to offering national radio exposure the job paid $75.00 a week, more than double what he was then making.

After singing two numbers for Lynn Murray, Shea was given a piece of music to learn. It was "Song of the Vagabonds" from Rudolph Friml's *The Vagabond King* which they were going to sing at the Texas Centennial. Included in its libretto was a line that made him uncomfortable. It read, ". . . and to hell with Burgundy." When he was a boy his Wesleyan Methodist preacher father would have washed his mouth out with soap for saying "shucks."

He took the music and left the studio but he didn't know what to do next. That night he prayed about it. He thought of the hurt he might bring to his father and family. He thought of his brother studying for the ministry and another brother who taught at a Christian college. He wondered what his next compromise might be. He prayed, "God, I don't know why you led me into this dilemma—maybe you're trying to test me. Anyway I'm not going to accept their offer if they make it. I can't think this is the way you'd have me serve you."

The next day Mr. Murray's secretary called and said, "Mr. Shea, congratulations, you are now one of the Lynn Murray Singers."

He swallowed hard and answered, "I thank you for the invitation, but have decided I won't be able to accept the job. Please thank Mr. Murray for me and tell him I appreciate this kind offer."

One of his friends did take the job. And it led to others like it. But also he seemed to drift further and further away from the church.[4]

Shea's first commitment was to Christ. This led to his other decisions.

In this statement to the Pharisees Jesus was not teaching against tithing. Neither am I. But I do want to see that we get some things in proper perspective. Tithing is not a substitute. Commitment is imperative.

[1] Robert J. Hastings, *My Money and God* (Nashville: Broadman Press, 1961), pp. 69-70. Reprinted by permission of the author.

[2] *Ibid.,* pp. 70-71.

[3] *Ibid.,* p. 87.

[4] George Beverly Shea, *Then Sings My Soul* (Old Tappan, N.J.: Fleming H. Revell Company, 1968), pp. 13-17. Reprinted by permission of the publisher.

# THE BASES FOR STEWARDSHIP

*I Corinthians 4:1-5*

We are always more vitally concerned with the things in which we have a part. The *Wall Street Journal* sometime ago called our attention to the fact that never in the history of America have so many people owned so many stocks or had as a great stake in American industry as now. They were elated over the large number of "little people," small investors, all having a part in American business. For instance, American Telephone and Telegraph Company which owns Western Union, the Bell Telephone system, Western Electric, and most of the telephone companies in the United States has 1,360,000 stockholders; in other words one out of twenty Americans owns stock in this company. Economists say that this is good for it gives us all an interest in the economy.

It is possible for each one of us to have a share in the greatest enterprise in the world—the kingdom of God. We have an opportunity to invest in something that insures a profit, the most important profit in the world.

The Lord offers this investment to us in both positive and negative terms; then He draws a conclusion. I like the way one translation renders it: "Do not be obsessed with the desire of treasuring up treasure for yourself." This does not mean that a person is not to be interested in taking care of his family or providing for the future. The Lord would want us to do that. But He says, "Do not be obsessed with the desire to store up treasure selfishly for yourself. But desire to lay up treasure in heaven where no one ever loses, where moth and rust doth not corrupt, nor thieves break in and steal. For where your treasure is there will your heart be also" (Matt. 6:19-21). Jesus is interested in everyone making this investment because Jesus is interested in everyone having his heart in the right place.

The word we usually use to describe this investment is

*stewardship.* The text says "moreover it is required in stewards that a man be found faithful." It is a very interesting word. A steward is strictly "the manager of a household or household affairs." He is one to whom the head of the house or proprietor has entrusted the management of his affairs. Stewardship, then, is the management of a household or household affairs. It is caring for the affairs of others. This investment that we are to make, then, is actually the proper care of what has been entrusted to us by another—God. This helps us to understand the basis of stewardship. In thinking of the basis of stewardship we should look at it from three angles: the Biblical basis, the practical basis, and the personal basis.

## THE BIBLICAL BASIS

The Biblical basis for stewardship is that God owns all things. Notice a few of the Biblical statements: "the land is mine [God's]" (Lev. 25:23); "the earth is the Lord's" (Ps. 24:1); "Every beast . . . the cattle on a thousand hills [are God's]" (Ps. 50:10); "the silver . . . and the gold is mine [God's] (Hag. 2:8).

The Bible man has no trouble with stewardship. He has the constant awareness that everything in the world is God's. If God could create the world then He owns the world. Because of His ownership the land was not even to be sold out of Israel. It is God's and God just lets us use it.

The Biblical basis for stewardship is that God owns us: "all souls are mine" (Ezek. 18:4); "we are the Lord's" (Rom. 14:8); "ye are not your own . . . bought with a price" (I Cor. 6:19-20).

The people of the Old Testament lived always under the shadow of the Exodus. Could they refuse God anything? He had found them a little group of slaves and had delivered them and made them a mighty nation.

Christians live always under the shadow of the Cross. Can we refuse God anything? He found us depraved, powerless sinners. With His own blood He bought us and made us a people. How tragic it would be were we ever to forget this.

The Biblical basis for stewardship, then, rests solidly on two pillars. The one is the ultimate ownership of God of everything. The other is the ownership of God of even our own lives. We can do no less, for God has done so much. Because God owns it we are just His stewards. As faithful stewards we do nothing but return to Him that which He has claimed for His own use.

## THE PRACTICAL BASIS

The practical *fact* is that the church needs money to operate.

Just as it takes money to operate your home, a business, or a government so does it take money to operate a church. God has ordained that those who serve the churches should receive their living from the churches. That means that salaries have to be paid. Buildings have a maintenance expense just as your house does. Utility bills must be paid. Literature has to be bought. We need to take our place in worldwide missions. All of this takes money. If we are to have a church that operates we will have to have money to operate it.

Someone always says, "Why doesn't the preacher preach the gospel and not preach on money?" The answer is that there is no such thing as preaching the gospel without preaching money. Money and the spread of the gospel are closely linked. One reason we have not done more in the spreading of the gospel around the world is that we have not had more money with which to do it.

If a person comes under the power of the gospel and is converted, then this will touch his money too. We say that one's Christianity is to pervade every area of his life. But if that is true—and it is—then that means it is to touch his pocketbook too. There is no such thing as New Testament Christianity that doesn't touch the pocketbook and make us want to give.

The practical fact is that we must have money if the church and the kingdom of God are to function. The practical fact is that our work in our communities has actually been grievously hampered because we have not had the money that we need. We have not been able to take the place that should be ours. The practical fact is that preaching the gospel involves preaching money for the gospel. If it means anything to you it will affect your giving. It is also a fact that the gospel can't be spread unless there is the necessary money to make this possible.

The practical question is, "When is the time to start giving?"

You say, "I don't make much money." "I have a lot of bills to pay." "I am in debt." "I just barely get by as it is." All of that may be true but it really has little bearing on this matter of our Christian responsibility of giving to God. For everyone who says, "I don't make much money," I can point you to one who makes less money and still tithes. For everyone who says, "I have a lot of bills to pay," I can point you to one who has as many bills to pay and still tithes. For everyone who says, "I am in debt," I can point you to one who is in debt and still tithes.

The greatest tithing testimony I ever observed was when I was waiting to see the manager of a grocery store. An old widow came in and asked the store owner to cash her old age assistance check for $55. He asked her how she wanted it and she replied "It doesn't make any difference just so I have a five-dollar bill and a fifty-cent piece." As he gave her the money she explained as she tucked the half-dollar wrapped up in the five-dollar bill into the corner of her purse, "This is my tithe. I put it separate so I won't spend it." She wasn't making much, she had bills to pay, and more than likely she was in debt, but she was tithing her income to God. The question then resolves itself not to "Can I give?" but "When will I start giving?"

It's easy to look at a person and say, "If I had as much money as he does I would tithe." The truth of the matter is that if you don't tithe now you probably wouldn't if you had as much money as he does. You have to start tithing when you have little if you are going to tithe when you have much.

It is harder to give ten dollars out of a hundred than it is to give ten thousand dollars out of a million. The man who has the great problem in giving is not the man who has the great sums of money but the small sums. But if people start giving properly to the Lord they usually start when they have small sums.

In June of 1955 Wayne Causey, an eighteen-year-old boy from Monroe, Louisiana, signed with the Baltimore Orioles baseball team as a "bonus baby." He received a $30,000 bonus to be paid over a three-year period. When he sent his check for $1,150, the tithe of the first payment, to the College Place Baptist Church in Monroe it made headlines. What the headlines didn't say was that the summer before he had cut the grass of that same church for $5 a week and had tithed 50¢.

I am telling you these things not to make you think that if you tithe you will get a $30,000 bonus or become a millionaire but to show you that if you are ever going to tithe you will have to start while you are not making much money or you won't do it when you make a lot of money.

## THE PERSONAL BASIS

It gives us a sense of stewardship. Do you remember the sense of importance you had when you drove a car for the first time? You felt that you were very important as you controlled all that power.

The sense of stewardship is of that nature. It is actually a great blessing to know that you are a manager, a steward for God in this great enterprise.

Great preachers throughout the years have recognized this sense of stewardship; it isn't just a new thing:

Chrysostom in the second century: "It is a shame that we who are Christians treat so lightly, under grace, that which the Jew took so seriously under law."

Augustine in the fifth century: "We allowed the Heathen to give so much more to their idols and their gods of wood and stone, and to give it so sacrificially, that it put to shame those of us who claim to worship, honor and love the living God."

Spurgeon in the nineteenth century: "Much of the unhappiness and discontent in the lives of many Christian people is their basic dishonesty when it comes to their honoring God with their substance."

It gives us a sense of partnership.

In a very real sense we are a partner in all that our money does. Whenever the pastor preaches or witnesses or visits in the hospital you are there.

Whenever the minister of music leads the choir in a worship

number you are there with him. Whenever the janitors clean the building you are there with them. Whenever a missionary preaches, teaches, or heals you are there. Whenever a seminary or Christian college instructs young people you are there. Whenever a Christian hospital saves a life you are there. Whenever a Christian children's home takes in a parentless child you have placed your arms around that babe. Whenever a tract or Sunday school lesson leads a person to Christ you have spoken through it.

It is a tremendous partnership that comes through giving.

In North Carolina there was a Baptist deacon whose pastor called him in one day for a conference. In substance he said to the deacon: "There is a young man from one of our finest Christian homes who feels definitely the call to be a missionary. His family cannot afford to send him through college, so I am not going to mince words with you. I am going to level with you. You are wealthy. I think God wants you to see him through. Will you do it?"

Without a moment's hesitation, the answer came back, "Yes, sir, Pastor, I'll do it."

The pastor sat with his mouth hanging open in astonishment. The deacon began to chuckle. "You thought you were going to have to do some selling, didn't you? You thought you were going to have to use some pressure and persuasion, didn't you? You weren't expecting me to say right off, 'Yes, I'll finance him through college and the seminary.' Well, let me tell you why I answered so fast. God is giving me a second chance. Fifteen years ago God sent the preacher to me with the same proposition, and I turned him down. That boy I didn't help is one of the grandest preachers today that I have ever heard, and I cry every time I hear him preach because I could be standing behind him in the pulpit wherever he goes, if I hadn't said No to God. Sure, I'll send your missionary. Who is he?" The pastor answered. "Theron Rankin is the boy. Theron Rankin." Theron Rankin spent years as a missionary in China, later was regional secretary for the Orient, and then executive secretary of the Foreign Mission Board of the Southern Baptist Convention.[1] This deacon was his partner in all that he did.

It gives us a sense of obedience.

This is the real key to stewardship. We give out of a heart of love and obedience to Christ. I never read II Corinthians 8:5 without feeling a shiver of thrill. Real stewardship is not giving just money, but giving yourself to the Lord. If God can't have you He doesn't want your money. But if God has you then He will also have your money. This is the big thing about stewardship. It is so pervasive. There is no area of life that can get away from it. It includes all that you are.

Obedience is the personal quality in stewardship. George W. Truett once said: "The true wealth of an individual is determined by what a man would have left if his money were all swept away."

What would you have left? Would you still have a life dedicated to God? Would you still have obedience to the Lord? That is real stewardship.

Warren C. Hultgren told of sitting in the Driscol Hotel in Corpus Christi, Texas, with Charles R. Moore, who was a senior deacon in the Cliff Temple Baptist Church, Dallas, Texas. Mr. Moore built the twenty-five million dollar Dangerville Dam. He was the chairman of the board of seven different subsidiary companies of the Austin Bridge Company. He was number-two man during the Second World War on the War Production Board. During a dinner he told of making twenty-five dollars a month when he first got married. They paid twelve dollars of that for the home in which they lived. When they came to that home, he and his wife agreed that 10 percent of everything they ever made they would give to God. He said, "We first gave God a tenth, then we gave God a fourth, then gave God a half, and," he said, "last year seventy-five cents of every dollar we gave, through our church, to the work of Christ." Then his wife said, "Brother Hultgren, we might as well tell you the truth. If we lost every dime that we ever made tomorrow, we would never regret a penny we have given to Christ, because Charlie and I know that the only thing we have to our name is what we have given to God over the years."

This is the basis for stewardship. Not that we would have a big figure to put in the church records but that we might have a partnership and a fellowship in the work of God; that we might treasure up treasures in heaven; that we might know that we have proved our love and obedience to God. Stewardship is based on the fact that Christ loved us and gave Himself for us. It grows out of the fact that we love Him and give to Him.

[1] C. Roy Angell, *The Price Tags of Life* (Nashville: Broadman Press, 1959), pp. 105-106. Used by permission.

# WHERE DO WE BEGIN IN CHRISTIAN STEWARDSHIP?

*II Corinthians 8:5*

"Well begun is half done," we have often heard. Anyone who has ever entered a race knows the importance of a good start. All other things being equal the person who has a good start, a good beginning, will win the race.

But as with so many other things, one of our most perplexing problems is knowing how to get off to a good start, how to begin. We want to live a life of love and practice love, but where do we begin? We want to be good witnesses for Christ, but where do we begin? We want to be good stewards, to practice stewardship, but where do we begin?

Paul gave us a good suggestion on where to begin in Christian stewardship when he discussed the action of the people of Macedonia. Paul had been engaged in a special collection for the Christian church at Jerusalem. This was the mother church for all Christians. But the church was poor. The people had felt the pressure of persecution. Now they had known the pinch of poverty. To the Christians at Corinth, Paul gave the example of the Christians at Macedonia; from their own poverty they gave with a spirit of joy and liberality. But something else was more important, first they gave themselves.

We often have some mistaken notions about the teaching of Christian stewardship. Some think it is only an effort to get money for the church. Some think that it is an attempt to increase from year to year the amount of money a church receives. Actually, this is only a part of it. The real goal is to develop a feeling of stewardship of all of life, of absolute accountability to God. The Macedonians were not satisfied with fragmentary giving, of separating the gift from the giver. And neither should we be. This is where we begin in Christian stewardship—with the gift of self.

The first step is the decision to accept Christ as Savior of the life. In Christian stewardship we begin with decision.

# DECISION

We see our need, our sin, our failure. This can only lead us to Christ, to make our decision for Him.

Years ago in London a young and skeptical medical student attended a revival being conducted by Dwight L. Moody. His motive in attending was to "see what a Yankee evangelist looks like." Like a trip hammer, the words of the preacher reverberated, "Let God have your life, let God have your life, let God have your life!" The cynical student grasped the meaning of the dedicated life. Thousands now remember him as Sir Wilfred Grenfell, missionary doctor to the neglected people of Labrador.

Grenfell began with decision and went on to full stewardship of his life and abilities. We must begin at the same place.

Without definite decision for Jesus Christ the teaching of stewardship is futile. Without the acceptance of Jesus Christ as Lord of life the appeal to stewardship is empty. It is something akin to wishful thinking to expect persons who have never decided for Christ to follow Christ in stewardship.

Christian stewardship is a Christian endeavor. One cannot embark upon Christian endeavors without Christ. The way to receive Christ is by decision: the commitment of one's total life to Christ in faith.

Where do we begin in Christian stewardship? We begin right where the Macedonians began: by giving ourselves to God in faith commitment.

# DEDICATION

When we accept Jesus Christ as Savior we also accept Him as Lord. These are not two separate decisions. Where do we begin in Christian stewardship? We begin with dedication.

Dedication to God is the key to Christian stewardship. This assures us that the decision for giving has already been made.

If one has dedicated his life to Christ some decisions do not have to be made anew each time the issue arises. The decision has already been made. The Christian should not have to fight the battle over whether he will cheat, gamble, be unfaithful to his mate, lie, steal, or live without personal integrity.

These decisions should have already been made when he gave his life to Christ.

The kind of dedication that recognizes Jesus Christ as Lord of life and acknowledges individual acountability to God for all that we have and are should not really have to labor through the problem of Christian stewardship. That decision should already have been made.

This in turn says some other things about money: how we make it and how we spend it. Voltaire once said: "When it comes to money everybody has the same religion." But that is not right.

In his book *My Money and God* Robert J. Hastings has collected some examples in which religion and business have been mixed.

A buinessman was offered a deal to make a great sum of quick money. He declined the offer, giving Christian principles as his reason. His friend countered, "Surely you can't try to mix two good things like business and religion." He answered, "I have discovered that it is only when we do mix business and religion that we can *prove* our religion and *improve* our business!"

As a young man, J. C. Penney invested his savings in a butcher shop. He was advised to buy a bottle of whiskey each week for the chef of the local hotel, his best customer. He purchased a bottle the first week, then quit when he became convicted it was wrong. He lost his business but won his self-respect and later made a fortune in retail selling.

Then there was the Christian fish merchant in Boston many years ago who formed a partnership with some other men to buy up all the codfish brought into their harbor. Then they raised the prices and sat back to wait for a killing. But in a few days the Christian partner broke up the deal. He explained, "When I knelt in prayer at family altar, a whole mountain of codfish rose between me and God as I thought of the poor people who were going hungry. Gentlemen, I would not let all the fish in the Atlantic Ocean come between me and the Lord."

And we are reminded of the old Scot who was pressured

by a local committee to sell liquor in his store. They threatened boycott if he refused. He replied, "I want you to know, gentlemen, that my goods are for sale, but not my character."

A man of many business interests in Prichard, Alabama, was converted. One of his holdings was a beer distributorship, which the previous year had netted him $67,000. One of the first things he did was to sell it. He explained, "I cannot claim to be a Christian and have beer trucks driving over town with my name on the sides."

And a lawyer said, "I had to quit serving a particular insurance company because of its demand that I pressure claimants into settling for less than they deserved."

Examples could be multiplied of men who do mix religion and business, who do face the inevitable conclusion that stewardship begins with how the dollar gets into a man's pocketbook, and not with the dollars that go into the collection basket on Sunday. In the face of multiplied temptations to make a quick or unethical dollar, they are determined to honor God first by giving a full measure of service for every dollar received.[1]

## DESIGN

Where do we begin in Christian stewardship? We begin with design. The design God has for your life is for your whole life, not just your money.

Back in 1939, when the Nazis were at the height of their power in Germany, the following poem appeared in a Berlin newspaper. It signified the militant, aggressive desire of dictatorship to conquer the *wills* of men as well as their *bodies:*

> We have captured all the positions
> And on the heights we have planted
> The banners
> Of our revolution.
>
> You had imagined
> That was all
> That we wanted.
>
> We want more.
> We want all!
> Your hearts are our goal,
> It is your souls we want![2]

The struggle for men's souls still goes on. Nazism may be dead, but many other things that clamor for attention and claim the souls of men still are very much in evidence. Materialism may be the chief claimant. Materialism assumes that true happiness can be found in the *things* that one has amassed. The things available are paraded before us and the "good life" is constantly promoted. The advertisers make sure that we know what we can have for our own comfort and to stoke the fires of our egos. The incessant cry seems to be:

Your hearts are our goal,
It is your souls we want.

But there is another, and stronger, claim on the souls of men. This is God's call to us. God has His designs on the souls of men. This is God's goal—He wants your hearts and lives.

Why does God want your lives? Hastings said it: "God does not want to exploit, but to bless us. He does not want to dominate, but to lead. Neither does he want to crush, but to heal; nor to destroy self-respect and human individuality, but to raise man to his highest potential. We are his children. He is our Father. He wants the best for us. But before he gives us *his* best, we must give him *our* lives."[3]

Where do we begin in Chrisitan stewardship? Why, we begin at the very place those early Christians in Macedonia began. We begin by giving our lives to God in faith, trust, and commitment. Any other starting point is futile. This is where Christian stewardship begins: with our lives given in dedication and love to God.

[1] Robert J. Hastings, *My Money and God* (Nashville: Broadman Press, 1961), pp. 28-29. Reprinted by permission of the author.

[2] *Ibid.,* p. 9.

[3] *Ibid.,* p. 10.

## THE SPIRIT OF STEWARDSHIP

*Mark 12:41-44*

When Charles A. Lindbergh captured the heart and imagination of the United States and the world by being the first man to fly across the Atlantic alone, he did it in a little plane named "The Spirit of St. Louis." I've seen that plane. It is hanging from the ceiling in one of the rooms in the Smithsonian Institution in Washington, D.C. You would wonder how he could even fly across the state in that thing, to say nothing of flying across uncharted oceans.

But it is the name of the plane we want to think about now—"The Spirit of St. Louis." It was named for the people of St. Louis, Missouri, who had helped and supported him. The spirit of the man seemed to capture the spirit of the people. It was a spirit of adventure, bravery, and courage. This word *spirit* is often used in this sense. It refers to the essence, the heart, the temper, the disposition of a thing.

In this sense it is proper to talk about the spirit of stewardship. What is the heart of stewardship, the disposition that would cause a person to give of himself and his substance to a cause? Stewardship we understand to mean the management or administration of what has been placed in our trust. So this word implies two things: it implies trust, and it implies management. The Lord has entrusted us with many things: health, life, talents, money. The question then is: How are we going to manage these things? What are we going to do with the things the Lord has entrusted to us?

About the best Biblical picture of the spirit of stewardship is found in the story of the widow's mite. Jesus told this story Tuesday before the crucifixion. It was His last public act before His arrest. The day had been a busy one for Jesus. He had been in controversy with both the Pharisees and the Sadducees.

Now He was sitting alone. Probably He was sitting near the Gate Beautiful watching the people as they placed an offering in one of the thirteen "trumpet boxes" in the Court of the Women. Only one of the gifts drew a comment from Him. This was the gift of a widow. Jesus called attention to this act not because of the amount of the gift, but because of the spirit in which it was given. He said that the others had given of their abundance—other translations use the word *superfluity,* more than enough—but she had given all that she had, even her living. It was the spirit of this woman's stewardship that made the difference.

In this incident we can see the spirit of stewardship.

## MOTIVE

The spirit of stewardship involves the motive for giving.

Notice that Jesus was sitting near the treasury. He was watching *how* the people gave. This shows us that it was not the amount that mattered but the motive and the spirit behind the gift.

The thirteen trumpet-shaped boxes were located in the Court of the Women. This was a general court. Each of the boxes was designated for some use: incense, wood, oil, food for the poor, clothing for the destitute. They were divided between the needs of the Temple and the needs of the people. Now because these trumpets were metal a person could come in and parade by them and very conspicuously place money in the containers. What was their motive: to show off and parade their giving or to give as an act of worship to relieve human need?

I think that we need to examine our motives for giving. I think that the Scripture definitely teaches that the tithe is the minimum gift a Christian should give.

But why do we tithe? Is it in a legalistic sense—I have to do it? Is it out of fear—I must do it or God will take it away from me? Is it for gain—If I tithe then I will have more?

I think that all of these are inferior motives for giving money to the church and for God's use. The real motive for giving should be out of gratitude to God for His grace and as an act of worship. We should give because we recognize that Christ has given all for us. Since Christ has saved us and allowed us to live, since all that we have comes from God, since we realize that what we have in this world is only that which is held in trust—then certainly we ought to honor that trust and give with a clean heart and a proper motive. As an act of worship based on love—this is the way we ought to give.

Two wealthy Christians, a lawyer and a businessman, joined in a round-the-world tour. In Korea one day they saw in a field by the side of the road a boy pulling a crude wooden plow, while an old man held the plow handles and guided it through the rice paddy.

The lawyer was quite surprised and took a snapshot of the scene. "That's a curious sight. I suppose they are very poor," he said to the missionary, who was their interpreter and guide.

"Yes," was the quiet reply, "that's the family of Chi Novi. When the church was built after the war, they were eager to share in its construction but had no money. So they sold their only ox and gave the money to the church. This spring they are pulling the plow themselves."

The lawyer and businessman by his side were quiet for a few minutes. Then the businessman remarked, "That must have been a real sacrifice."

"They did not call it that," said the missionary. "They felt fortunate to have an ox to sell."

The two tourists had little to say; but when they reached home, the lawyer took the picture to his pastor and told him of the incident that had so impressed him. "I intend to double my giving through my church—and I want you to give me some plow work to do. I have never given anything to Christ that really cost me anything! I had to go around the world to learn that."

When are we going to learn?

## PURPOSE

Motive tells us something about *how* we give. Purpose tells something about *why* we give. J. Wallace Hamilton defined *stewardship* thus: "This is what the New Testament means by 'stewardship' that divine alchemy by which money is transmuted into men, and material possessions exchanged for the riches of mind and spirit."[1]

Quite often churches will increase facilities, increase the paid staff, and enlarge the program without ever really increasing the level of giving. This sometimes causes problems.

A very practical purpose for giving then arises: the needs must be met. Increasing ministry can very seldom result without increased financial support.

Another purpose for our giving is the sense of partnership that it gives us. When we give our money to the cause of Christ then we know that we have had a part in all that is done through this. Our giving gives us each an opportunity to preach, teach, and heal throughout the world.

For many years J. B. Tidwell was chairman of the Religion Department of Baylor University. In this position he influenced a whole generation of Texas Baptist preachers. Life had not always been easy for Tidwell. In his early days of marriage and ministry, while attempting to get an education to prepare himself for the Lord's service, he had a hard struggle. Robert A. Baker described it in *J. B. Tidwell Plus God,* a biography.

These hardships did three things for him. They taught him, for one thing, a lesson of God's providence that became a part of his outlook on life. During his second year in college, so many distressing financial crises arose that they became almost continuous. This was one of the years that the family had no meat on the table, save on those rare occasions when they happened to be given a chicken, or even more rare, when they bought one. One week they were badly in need of sheets for the home. As J. B. left the house, his wife mentioned again their need, expressing a hope that in some way they could get some unbleached muslin from which she could make the sheets. He replied that he did not have the two dollars required for this purchase, but would try to get credit for that amount. His wife suggested that he go by the post office first. Although he had no particular reason to do so, he did stop there, and received a letter from a man living at Cleveland, Alabama, whom he had known very slightly. The letter, giving evidence that the writer was uneducated, read about as follows:

Dear Brother J. B.: I have been thinking a great deal about you lately. Know you are having an awfully hard time. I am a very poor man. Don't have much. But I have been trying to pray for you every day and I wish I was able to help you a lot but I am not. But I am enclosing a little bit that may be some help in a tight.

Albert Head

Enclosed was a two-dollar bill, just enough to buy the domestic.

Tidwell later said:

Almost ten years later I returned to my home community to preach a commencement sermon at a little college. The people had come from miles around to see what I now looked like. I spied Albert Head out in the audience. He had ridden ten miles on horseback to hear me preach. I have many times wondered in thinking back that if I have ever done any good in Texas, how much may be credited to that good man. He followed me with prayers and sympathy as well as the gift. In the plan of God He allows people to be rewarded jointly. I prayed that day that God would give him some little dividend on his investment. Nothing in all my experience has stimulated me more to want to be something than the confidence which was indicated by that little assistance that was given me in those difficult days.[2]

## COMMITMENT

To give our money means that we have already committed ourselves to God. Jesus commended the widow because she gave to the point of sacrifice, she gave her living. The others gave out of their abundance. The spirit of stewardship involves commitment.

We cannot read this story without a sense of shame. We usually give like the others who gave—out of an abundance. By that I don't mean that we all have so much money that we don't miss what we give to the church or to the Lord. But I mean that we usually do not do without other things in order to be able to give to our Christ.

In 1965, according to National Council of Churches figures, the average per capita gift of church members in forty-four denominations was $77.75. This is about $1.48 per week.

79

I doubt that the level has increased a great deal since then.

Most of us drink more coffee and cokes than that. We spend much more than that on entertainment. We spend more than that to take care of our lawns during the summer.

*Commitment reflects importance.* We don't give as much to Christ as to these other things simply because we usually do not think them as important. An adequate financial church program is built on gifts from systematic, regular tithers; not on receipts from special drives or the infrequent donations of a few big givers.

*Commitment reflects concern.* If we are concerned with the trust that is ours then we will fufill it and give. There is a real sense of obligation imposed on the Christian when he comes to realize that all he has is from God. If we have concern and obligation then it will show in our commitment.

The late Douglas Freeman published a letter which General Jackson wrote to his pastor in Lexington, Virginia, soon after the first Battle of Bull Run in July, 1861. Having heard of the bloody fighting, the people of Lexington were anxious for details, and especially word concerning their sons and neighbors who had gone to war under the command of the former Virginia Military Institute professor.

At last a letter came to the Presbyterian minister in the handwriting of Jackson. Holding it high the preacher announced, "Gather around and I shall read you the news." The crowd became quiet as the preacher read aloud:

> My dear Pastor: In my tent last night, after a fatiguing day's service, I remembered that I had failed to send you my contribution for our colored Sunday school. Enclosed you will find my check for that object, which please acknowledge at your earliest convenience, and oblige.
>
> > Yours faithfully,
> > T. J. Jackson

There was not a word about the battle. At the close of "a fatiguing day's service" he remembered his church pledge. May the good example of Stonewall Jackson remind each of us to keep our church obligations.

*Commitment reflects your life.* That is what I mean by

commitment really—your life. I am convinced that what Christ really wants is your life. The widow was able to give her money because she had already given her heart. If your heart and life are in God's hands then I am not really concerned with your money—that will follow.

This is the spirit of stewardship: motive, purpose, commitment. An individual can only catch the spirit of stewardship when he has caught the spirit of Christ.

[1] J. Wallace Hamilton, *Ride the Wild Horses!* (Westwood, N.J.: Fleming H. Revell Company, 1952), p. 61. Reprinted by permission of the publisher.

[2] Robert A. Baker, *J. B. Tidwell Plus God* (Nashville: Broadman Press, 1942), pp. 36-40. Reprinted by permission of the author.

# PART II
# SOME STEWARDSHIP STORIES

# ... CONCERNING WHAT TO GIVE

## GIVING OUR BEST TO GOD

A missionary woman in India met a Hindu woman one morning to whom she had tried to witness several times. She was carrying two Hindu children in her arms. One was a beautiful, intelligent child, healthy and promising. The older child had a crippled, twisted body; and her mind was just as deficient as her body. The missionary asked the Hindu woman where she was going and received the astounding reply: "I'm on my way to the river to offer one of children to our gods as a sacrifice for my sin."

Once again the missionary witnessed to the woman, but to no avail.

Some days later she again met the woman. This time she was carrying only the deformed child. Anxiously, the missionary inquired about the other child only to hear the reply: "Why, don't you remember? When I saw you last, I told you I was on my way to the river to offer one of my children to the gods."

"Oh, my friend!" cried the missionary. "If you had to offer one of your children, why did you not throw this child into the river—this one who never will be well or intelligent?"

In utter astonishment, the Hindu replied: "Well, maybe that is the way you do in your religion; but in our religion, we give the best that we have to our gods."

Joseph B. Underwood, *By Love Compelled* (Nashville: Broadman Press, 1966), pp. 109-110. Reprinted by permission of the author.

## A CHRISTIAN SCANDAL

Representatives of twenty-three churches (including the Roman Catholic) from thirty countries recently convened at Bossey, near Geneva, to consider the Christian Attitude to Money. Ministers and laymen, economists and educationalists, theologians and church executives, accountants and businessmen gave long hours each day through worship and Bible study, lecture and discussion, to discover God's will for his people in this matter of such significance. They called it a scandal that the Church at the present time wastes so much money on the maintenance of institutions which no longer serve its life and mission. They also said, "It is no less a scandal that in affluent societies the giving of church members bears no proper relationship to their mounting disposable incomes." Any table of statistics bears out this depressing fact. According to figures published by the government, the average Englishman, after he has paid the rent and bought his food and clothing and spent the usual amount on alcohol, tobacco and entertainment, gives so little of his increased income to God that it does not even deserve mention.

Leonard Griffith, *This Is Living* (Nashville: Abingdon Press, 1966), pp. 155-156. Reprinted by permission of the publisher.

## EXCHANGE CURRENCY FOR THAT CURRENCY ACCEPTABLE IN A NEW COUNTRY

When I came from Canada to this country I was very young. My sister, who came with me, was younger still. We were both as green as the country fields where, up to then, we had lived. We had heard a lot about Chicago—that awful, wicked city where gangsters lie in wait in dark alleys, and all eight-year-olds carry guns—and when we reached Chicago and walked out of the station into the roaring street, I kept my hand on my watch. I watched out for my sister, too. We were afraid to take a taxi from the station; we had heard that smart taxi-drivers would take country folk like us ten miles around the city in order to reach an address two blocks from the station, and run up a big bill (a rumor not wholly unfounded, I think!). So we lugged our heavy luggage abroad a streetcar. I handed the conductor a quarter—a perfectly good *Canadian* quarter; he handed it back, saying gruffly, "Counterfeit!" Something not quite Christian rose in me, and I felt like telling him something, but the crowd behind us was pushing to get on, so we scrambled off, luggage, quarter, and all—including our anger. Just for that, we wouldn't ride on his old streetcar, at any price. We lugged our heavy grips for twenty city blocks. I never did find out whether or not the city of Chicago was disappointed at losing our patronage that day, but the next day we exchanged our Canadian money for currency acceptable in the new country.

Do you see what I am driving at? We shall all shortly be moving to a new country—a country of the spirit, where there is nothing but spirit. *We had better become acquainted at the spiritual bank!*

J. Wallace Hamilton, *Ride the Wild Horses!* (Westwood, N.J.: Fleming H. Revell Company, 1952), pp. 63-64. Reprinted by permission of the publisher.

## "PIG TAIL" GIVING

C. E. Garrison once wrote about an intriguing custom among the natives of the New Hebrides. Missionaries report that as a part of the worship of the heathen gods in those islands, the natives roast and eat a pig—and then give the tail to their so-called god! How singularly appropriate: pig tail giving to a worthless deity. But we who worship the true and living God, the Lord Almighty, must know of our responsibility to give more.

C. E. Garrison in the church paper of the First Baptist Church, Altus, Oklahoma. Reprinted by permission.

## IF YOU CAN'T BE TRUSTED WITH MONEY, YOU CAN'T BE TRUSTED WITH OTHER THINGS

Dr. F. W. Boreham tells a terrible story of a meeting at which people were giving their testimonies. One woman sat silent. She was asked to make her testimony; she refused; from the look on her face it was easy to see that something was badly wrong. When she was asked what the matter was she answered that more than one of these other people who had just made glowing testimonies to Christ owed her money and her own family was near to starving. There could be no honesty or sincerity in testimonies like that. If we would use material things rightly we will neither worship them, nor yet despise them, but use them to bring strength, beauty and comfort to our own lives and to the lives of others.

William Barclay, *And Jesus Said* (Edinburgh: The Church of Scotland Department of Education, 1952), p. 142. Reprinted by permission of the publisher.

## WILL YOU LOOK INWARD OR OUTWARD?

I heard Dr. [Halford] Luccock say that while he was in Europe he visited two rooms that impressed him deeply. One was the Hall of Mirrors. In this hall, he could see nothing but repeated images of himself. In one nook he could see himself seven times at a single glance. But in a certain Swiss village, he went into another room that was so full of windows that he called it the "Room of Windows." Here he could not see one single image of himself. But his compensation for this loss was the fact that he could look out and see this wide world.

Clovis G. Chappell, *Sermons from the Miracles* (New York and Nashville: Abingdon Press, 1965 Apex Books), p. 224. Reprinted by permission of the publisher.

## REFUSAL TO LET MONEY GET BIGGER THAN GOD

It was my privilege for five years to be the pastor of a retired schoolteacher who had an enviable record of faithfulness to her church through her talents of time, influence, and money. Her twenty-five year record of teaching the third grade in public schools was almost matched by her service in teaching intermediate girls in Sunday school. Nothing was too good for her church, her pastor, her friends.

But the way had not been easy. Left a young widow with four small children, she entered a university to qualify for teaching so as to support her dependent family. There was financial struggle, but God always came first. One day her insurance man called, "Mrs. Hall, the premium on your house insurance is about due." Other bills were pressing. Something had to go unpaid, and it was the insurance.

Soon after, as she was walking home from her third grade

classroom, she noticed a fire truck and people gathered in the street near her home. She wondered whose house was afire. Her fears were justified, for it was her own. Doubly bad, her insurance had expired. She stood helplessly on the sidewalk watching the damage of smoke, fire, and water, as her furniture was dragged into the streets.

Before long her agent, attracted by the fire in the small town, drove up. He said quietly, "Mrs. Hall, do not worry about your home. Although it is against the recommendations of my company, I paid your premium the other day. Your insurance is in force. You will be paid for your loss."

This dear lady did not have such experiences every day, neither was her habit of life one of presumption on the mercy of God. But she had enough like experiences to cause me to ask, "Mrs. Hall, what has been the secret of your quiet faith through the years?" She did not hesitate a minute as she replied, "I have never allowed the dollar bill to get bigger than my God!"

Robert J. Hastings, *My Money and God* (Nashville: Broadman Press, 1961), p. 42. Reprinted by permission of the author.

## LOOKING AT MONEY IN TERMS OF HUMAN NEED

A missionary, home on furlough, was invited to a dinner at a summer resort where he met many women of prominence and position. Afterward, he wrote a letter to his wife: "Dear Wife: I've had dinner at the hotel. The company was wonderful. I saw strange things today. Many women were present, and some of them to my certain knowledge wore a church, 40 cottage organs, and 20 libraries."

In his great longing for money to provide Gospel for hungering millions, he could not refrain from estimating the silks, satins, and the diamonds of the guests at the dinner in terms of his people's needs.

J. Arthur Springer.

# . . . CONCERNING WHY TO GIVE

## OUR GOD IS A SOURCE OF INEXHAUSTIBLE TREASURE

Remember that the God to whom we give is not a public charity but a source of inexhaustible treasure. I know a minister who reminded his Church Council of that fact rather sharply. Irritated by their caution and their haggling over petty expenditure, he exclaimed, "How would you decide your policies if you knew that the Chairman of this business we are engaged in is the wealthiest person in the universe? Well, we do know that. God is our Chairman, God who is wealthy beyond all the world's millionaires put together. Let us decide and let us act as if we believed it!" To dramatize his conviction the minister vacated the chair at the head of the board-room table, and at future meetings he sat at the side, the chair remaining empty as a symbol of the presiding presence of God.

Leonard Griffith, *This Is Living* (Nashville: Abingdon Press, 1966), p. 158. Reprinted by permission of the publisher.

## THE PRICE OF SALVATION AND WHAT WE OWE IN RETURN

I have often regretted that I did not have the privilege of knowing the late Emil Mettler. He was a member of the City Temple, but he died shortly before I became the minister of that church. Mettler was a close friend and ardent supporter of Albert Schweitzer. The great missionary stayed with him when he visited Britain. Mettler owned a small restaurant in London where people remember him for a generosity which almost embarrassed them. Rarely would he allow a clergyman or any other Christian worker to pay for a meal. Once he happened to open his cash register in the presence of a Missionary Secretary. The Secretary was astonished to see among the bills and coins a six-inch nail. What was it doing there? "I keep this nail with my money," replied Mettler, "to remind me of the price that Christ paid for my salvation and of what I owe him in return."

Leonard Griffith, *God's Time and Ours* (London: Lutterworth Press, 1964), pp. 200-201. Reprinted by permission of the publisher.

## GOD'S GENEROSITY: OUR MOTIVE FOR GIVING

If Christian generosity has a motive, I suppose that motive would be the generosity of God. "What shall I render unto the Lord for all his benefits unto me?" It has been my experience in the ministry that when laymen take their religion seriously they require no urgent appeal for their money, but only an honest and intelligent presentation of the Church's need. There was a layman who once called me to his business office for that very purpose. I had just received him into Church membership, and now, as I carefully outlined the annual budget, I thought it might help him to know the average amount that church members gave. He sat back and looked at me in astonishment. "You and I are not thinking in the same terms at all," he said. "Joining the Church is one of the great decisions of my life, and it has to mean something. My annual gift will be . . . ," and he named a sum so substantial that it staggered me. "You are very generous," I murmured. He replied, simply, "God has been very generous to me."

Leonard Griffith, *God's Time and Ours* (London: Lutterworth Press, 1964), p. 198. Reprinted by permission of the publisher.

## GOD OWNS ALL THINGS

Leonard Sanderson in *Strength for Living* tells of making calls one afternoon with a young businessman while in an evangelistic crusade in Tulsa, Oklahoma. As they passed by a beautiful new office building Sanderson remarked, "That is a magnificent building."

He said, "Yes, that belongs to my father."

"Sure enough," Sanderson said, "You have every reason to be proud of that."

He referred to some other nice property during the afternoon, and each time the young businessman said, "That belongs to my father, too."

Sanderson said, "You are not pulling my leg, are you?"

He said, "No, I'm not kidding you, preacher. God is my father and he owns everything."

Leonard Sanderson, *Strength for Living* (Nashville: Broadman Press, 1969), p. 13. Used by permission.

## BE CAREFUL WHOM YOU ROB

An elderly Baptist deacon received an appointment to speak in a little church in the absence of the pastor. After the evening service he was handed two one-dollar bills. These he placed carefully in his billfold and started back to town afoot. As he entered the edge of the town he was suddenly confronted by a man with a big handkerchief over his face and a pistol in his hand.

"Give me your money," snarled the robber, "before I blow you in two with this gun."

Terrified the deacon shot both hands into the air as high as he could get them. Then he said, "Please, Mr. Robber, just reach into my back pocket and get my billfold out, but don't shoot me!"

The robber reached one hand around the trembling deacon and jerked out the billfold. Turning his light upon it, he opened it. He found the two one-dollar bills and a card. It was a card that had the deacon's name on it plus these words, "A Baptist Layman for Christ."

"Are you a member of a Baptist church?" questioned the robber.

"Yes, sir, I am a Baptist deacon and I do supply preaching."

"Well, here," said the robber. "Take this money back, I'm a Baptist myself."

All Baptists aren't that careful about whom they rob.

Baptists who do not give regularly through their church rob other Baptists of the ministry that the church can perform. As they shift more of the burden of financial support upon other church members they also rob them.

But they rob Baptists around the world too. Baptist work

in all the world suffers when an individual Baptist is not faithful financially.

And they rob themselves of the joys and privileges in participating through their money in exciting things for Christ.

But a prophet long ago really expressed it when he said, "Will a man rob God? Yet ye have robbed me. But ye say, Wherein have we robbed thee? In tithes and offerings."

When you start to make out your pledge card be careful whom you rob.

JEC

## SOMETHING TO REMEMBER
## WHEN YOU GIVE TO THE CHURCH

Harry Emerson Fosdick told of one of the major women's colleges which was conducting a financial campaign. A prominent alumna was asked by the committee to send a message to back up their appeal. "Make it gay," said the committee, "something to cheer us up." The alumna wrote back that she was glad to send a message but she would not make it gay. "Tell them this for me," she wrote. "Never take your college for granted! A lot of people broke their hearts to give it to you." Fosdick added, "That's true about the church."

That's true about the church universal. It is also true about our expression of the church whose building is located at 508 Second Street.

This one thought is what gives such meaning to the theme for our stewardship emphasis this year! "Give . . . in the spirit of Christ."

Christ gave His life for us. Surely in loving response to that great gift of grace we will give worthy gifts.

The worthy gift starts with the person. We must first give ourselves to Christ, then what monetary gift we should give will fall in place.

When we consider that a lot of people broke their hearts to give us our church, and that Christ gave His life to give

*94*

us our salvation, we cannot be flippant or unconcerned or smug about our Christian stewardship—we dare not!

JEC

## WORKING FOR GOD RATHER THAN WORKING FOR MONEY

There is no modern edition of this consuming zeal that Paul had. The closest of its kind has been recently written about an Australian bushman named Taylor. He has reclaimed about a hundred thousand acres of desert by digging wells and irrigation ditches. Green grass grows where hot sands once smothered all plant life. Someone asked him, "Why do you keep on living out in that hot desert? You are worth twenty-five million dollars. You do not need to work any more. Why don't you take life a little easier?"

His answer reminds me of Paul: "God commissioned me just as he commissioned every missionary and preacher in the world. He commissioned me to turn that desert into a beautiful place for people to live. Money? Money doesn't mean anything to me. I am not working for money, I am working for God. The money is nothing. As long as God lets me work, I will be turning desert sand into lush green vegetation."

C. Roy Angell, *God's Gold Mines* (Nashville: Broadman Press, 1962), pp. 108-109. Used by permission.

## OUR BUSINESS: EXTENDING THE KINGDOM OF GOD

When Carey first publicly presented his hopes for missions, a Brother Ryland brushed the topic aside with a rough, "Young man, sit down, sit down. When God pleases to convert the heathen, He'll do so without consulting you or me." Carey did not let the scoffs or rebuffs disquiet him. "For years," says S. P. Carey, "it burned in his bones; he felt the world's darkness." It is said that every night he kept adding to his own world map. He massed his data and cumulated his argument. The globe was his other Bible. The Bible began to throb with new meaning. He saw it as the progressive unfolding of God's world missionary purpose. When remonstrated for neglecting his business, he replied, "My business, my business! My business, sir, is to extend the kingdom of Christ. I only make and mend shoes to help pay expenses."

Joe L. Ingram in his sermon "He Hath Committed Unto Us the Word." Used by permission.

## WORTH MORE THAN MONEY

A young man was climbing rapidly to fame as a physician and diagnostician. His future was unusually bright, and the rungs of the ladder to success and fame seemed spaced advantageously for his own feet. In the very midst of this climb to professional power, he felt the call come to his heart to go to a foreign land as a medical missionary. His heart rebelled for a time, but the Voice of God was insistent and he finally surrendered to it.

One day after going as a medical missionary he said to a visiting minister. "If you would like to see a major operation be at the hospital at one o'clock." The minister stood on the balcony overlooking the operating table. The pitiless sun, beating on the roof of the hospital, and the ether fumes combined to give him a sense of nausea and he went out of the room to refresh himself.

He returned and the doctor was still operating. This he did four or five times, until seven long hours had passed. The last time he entered the operating room he noticed that the doctor had completed his last operation for the day. As they retired from the room, the minister said to him, "Doctor, is every day like this?"

The doctor looked at him. Beads of perspiration stood out on his forehead; his eyes were glassy; his lips were almost purple with the strain, and his hands began to tremble with fatigue. The minister said to him, "Doctor, how much would you have gotten for this operation in America?"

He replied, "Perhaps three or four hundred dollars . . . it was a complicated one." "How much will you receive for this?" the minister asked.

Looking at the poor native woman who had been wheeled into the operating room with only a copper in her hand, asking that in Christ's name he give her life, the doctor looked back at his friend and with tears welling up in those fine eyes and with a choke in his voice, he said, "Well, sir, for this I will get nothing but her grattitude and my Master's smile. But that, sir, is worth more than all the plaudits and money the world can give."

Sterling Price, "Obedience," taken from *Great Southern Preaching* edited by Gerald Martin, Copyright © 1969, by Zondervan Publishing House, Grand Rapids, Michigan, and is used by permission.

## WHAT EVER GETS YOUR ATTENTION GETS YOU

Whatever gets your attention gets you. If money, as an end, gets your attention, it gets you. A villager in India looked through the window of a dak bungalow (a government rest-house) and saw a European reading, seated before a candle stuck in a whisky bottle. The villager ran off to his village and announced, "Now I know what the white man worships—he worships the whisky bottle, for I saw him burn a light before it, and he had a book open in front of it and was saying his prayers to it!" There is just enough truth in that to make it sting. But while the modern man is less and less worshiping the whisky bottle, he is more and more saying to the Golden Calf of the material, "These be thy gods, O Israel, which brought thee up out of the land of Egypt." If the modern man doesn't worship the whisky bottle, he comes dangerously near worshiping the golden calf. We scorn the Hindu for worshiping the living cow, but is it any worse than worshiping a dead calf?

E. Stanley Jones, *The Christ of the Mount* (New York and Nashville: Abingdon Press, 1931), pp. 224-225. Reprinted by permission from the publisher.

## LEAVING THE WORLD WITH EMPTY HANDS

It is said that Alexander the Great gave instructions that when he died his body should be placed in the coffin in such a way that his hands were visible so that it should be seen that his hands were open—*and empty*. The conqueror of the world was well aware that he could take none of his conquests with him. It therefore follows that the supreme aim of life should not be the acquisition of merely temporary things but the formation of a self and of a character which some day we may take without shame to God.

William Barclay, *And Jesus Said* (Edinburgh: The Church of Scotland Committee on the Religious Instruction of Youth, 1952), p. 119. Reprinted by permission of the publisher.

## GIVING FROM GRATITUDE

The parents of a young man killed in the war gave their church a check for $200 as a memorial to their loved one. When the presentation was made, another war mother whispered to her husband, "Let's give the same for our boy."

"What are you talking about?" asked the father. "Our boy didn't lose his life."

"That's just the point," replied the mother. "Let's give it because he was spared."

Anonymous.

## GIVING TO HELP NEIGHBORS

A missionary on furlough in the United States was raising funds to carry on his work in a foreign land. He met one who did not believe in foreign missions. Said this man: "I want what I give to benefit my neighbors."

"How much land do you own?" the missionary asked.

"About five hundred acres."

"How far down do you own it?"

The man was stumped, but finally said that he supposed he owned to a depth "about half-way through the earth."

"Well," observed the missionary, "You had better give to me, then. I want this money for men whose land adjoins your land at the bottom."

Anonymous.

# GIVING FOR JESUS CHRIST

Andrew Fuller, a contemporary of William Carey, helped launch the modern movement of foreign missions on its way. It is said that one day he asked for a gift for missions from a friend in the community. Said his friend, "Well, Andrew, I'll give you five pounds, seeing it is you." "No," said Fuller, "I can't take anything for this cause, seeing that it is for me you are doing it." Feeling rebuked, the man hesitated a moment, then said, "Andrew, you are right, here are ten pounds seeing it is for the Lord Jesus Christ!"

Paul S. Rees, *The Adequate Man* (Westwood, N.J.: Fleming H. Revell Company, 1959), p. 118. Reprinted by permission of the publisher.

# ... CONCERNING HOW TO GIVE

## GRACIOUS GIVING FROM LITTLE

Luther Rice, seeking support for the Adoniram Judsons in Burma, hired two Negro slaves to row him down a river in Georgia. During the trip he had occasion to explain his mission. Upon conclusion of the trip, Rice began to make payment for services received, but the slaves refused to accept anything. Instead, they dug into their pockets and turned over everything to Rice—a total of twenty-five cents.

JEC

## THE TESTIMONY OF A GOOD MAN

"That was all we saved out of a mighty fortune ... it was what we gave away that we were able to keep forever." These words were the words of J. C. Stribling.

It was in 1933, following the great depression. I was pastor at Rotan. One day, coming down the street, I stepped up to the side of an old Ford car, worth then about $5, in which Mr. Stribling and his wife sat.

At one time Mr. Stribling owned many sections of west Texas ranch land. He had several thousand head of fine cattle. He owned stocks and bonds galore. It was during this time that he gave $150,000 to build Ruth Stribling Hall at Mary Hardin-Baylor College.

Then the depression came. He lost it all. When the clouds of complete failure began to clear the horizon, he did not have a cow, not an acre of ground, not a home, not even respectable clothing.

As he sat there in his little worn-out car wearing a cowboy hat that gave evidence of poverty I said, "Last week I took a car load of girls to Mary Hardin-Baylor College to enter school. I had the privilege of spending the night in the guest room of the beautiful dormitory that you gave on behalf of the Kingdom of God; and on behalf of Texas Baptists, let me thank you for this wonderful gift."

His eyes floated in tears. Slowly he placed his arm over the shoulders of his pioneer ranch wife and softly said, "That was all we saved out of a mighty fortune."

Presently he lifted himself as a victor and said, "Young preacher, tell men to give all they can to the Kingdom of God while they have it. I wish I had given more."

It is interesting that in the next few years this good man, toiling hard in the rattlesnake-infested land of the Double Mountain area of Fisher County, made a comeback. Again he buillt a mighty cattle empire.

J. D. Brannon, *Baptist Standard,* September 12, 1962. Reprinted by permission of the publisher.


## A SACRIFICIAL GIFT

Booker T. Washington, the great Negro educator who came up from slavery, personally raised over one million dollars for his famous Tuskegee Institute, built for the education of coloured people. His autobiography includes a chapter entitled "Raising Money" where he gratefully acknowledges the wealthy and generous benefactors who responded to his appeals. The chapter closes with the moving account of an old coloured lady, clad in rags and hobbling with the help of a cane, who came to him one day and said, "Mr. Washington, God knows I spent de bes' years of my life in slavery. God knows I's ignorant an' poor; but I knows what you an' Miss Davidson is tryin' to do. I knows you is tryin' to make better men and better women for de coloured race. I ain't got no money, but I want you to take dese six eggs which I'se been saving up, and I wants you to put dese six eggs into de eddication of dese boys and gals." Says Booker T. Washington, "Since the work at Tuskegee started, it has been my privilege to receive many gifts for the benefit of the institution, but never any, I think, that touched me so deeply as this one."

Leonard Griffith, *God's Time and Ours* (London: Lutterworth Press, 1964), pp. 199-200. Reprinted by permission of the publisher.

## THE REVERSED VERSION OF STEWARDSHIP

We sometimes hear of people who are so stubborn that we feel that they were born in the "objective case." If they should drown in the river, we would journey upstream to look for the body. Their usual and normal reaction is "negative." In response to a pastor's stewardship sermonette on tithing, just before the morning offering, a worshiper anonymously scribbled this note and put it on the offering plate: "Please explain—many don't pay their bills but religiously pay their tithe and possibly offerings. What is more important? Some of these owe me considerable." The pastor's Scriptural reply was John 21:21, 22, "Peter seeing him [John] saith to Jesus, Lord, and what shall this man do? Jesus saith unto him, If I will that he tarry till I come, what is that to thee? Follow thou me." The Lord Jesus "in the days of his flesh" gave little aid or sympathy to the worshiper who got so worried about his brother's sin.

The instance makes us think of the colporteur's experience who called at the farmhouse. When an old lady came to the door he asked, "May I sell you a Bible, Madam." "My, bless you," she replied, "we have more Bibles now in the house than we use. We have the Old Testament Bible, the New Testament Bible, the Holy Bible, and besides, we have the Reversed Version Bible also." Many Christians are faithful to that Reversed Version of the Bible. The Bible says, "Go ye . . . ," and they all with one accord and singleness of heart stay at home. The Bible says, "Thou shalt not covet . . . ," and they all together agree that it means "Thou shalt not give. . . ."

Reprinted from "The Reflector," the bulletin of the First Baptist Church of Jonesboro, Louisiana.

## WILLINGNESS TO GIVE TO GOD

Bishop Arthur Moore, of the Methodist Church, held a revival in the First Methodist Church in Baton Rouge during my pastorate in that city. He told of this incident from his own life. "I was preaching in a revival in a city not far away, and I noticed that on the back seat at each service was one of the most miserable-looking men I ever saw. He never opened a hymnbook or took any part in the service. He slipped down in the seat till his chin rested on his chest, with unhappiness written all over his face. During one of the services I asked the pastor, in a whisper, what was his trouble. He answered, 'It's a good story. You ask *him* that question.' "

The bishop said: "I slipped around to the door while the benediction was being said and stopped the man as he was hurrying out. In a gentle voice I asked him, 'Why are you so miserable? Won't you tell me what's the matter?" He answered about like this: 'Bishop, I want to be a Christian worse than anything in the world almost, but here's my trouble. I was brought up in Chicago, sleeping in boxcars about all of the time, while on the lake beautiful yachts lay anchored. And the rich people living in them threw overboard scraps that made me drool. Sometimes I got so mad I couldn't see, and I vowed that one day when I grew up I was going to anchor my own yacht out there, and it was going to be the biggest yacht on the lake. Today I am in a position to make that dream come true, or I will be in a few weeks. I am a rich man, and I own two big farms in Kansas. When the crops are harvested, I am going to sell them and the farms and buy that yacht.'

"The man seemed to have finished his story, and I looked at him and finally asked, 'Well, what has that to do with your being a Christian?' With surprise written all over his face, he said: 'Don't you see, if I surrender my life to God, he might want me to sell those farms and crops and give the money to missions. Wouldn't he?' " Bishop Moore said: "It was my turn to be surprised, and I finally said, 'He might or he might not, but, anyway, you ought not to accept his salvation and redemption until you are willing to give God all that you are and all

*104*

that you have, if he wants it.' A few days later, when the invitation hymn was being sung, he walked down the aisle with firm steps and knelt at the altar. I knelt by him. His prayer was perfect, 'Dear Lord, you can have the farms and the crops, you can have everything I own, and you can have me if you will forgive my sins and give me peace in my heart.'

"In the services after that he sat near the front, peace and joy in his countenance as he sang the hymns at the top of his voice. On the last day a Western Union telegraph boy brought him a telegram and handed it to him on the porch of the church. As he read it, he just said, 'Humph!' I asked him if it was bad news, and he handed me the telegram. It was from the manager of his farms in Kansas, and it read: 'Millions of grasshoppers out here. We have kept them off with fires and drums and tin pans. Come immediately and take charge. I won't accept further responsibility.' I said to him, 'Are you going?' He answered, 'No.' I asked, 'Why not?' "I gave those farms and those crops to the Lord. They belong to him. The grasshoppers belong to him, too. If he wants to pasture his grasshoppers on his corn and wheat, that's all right with me.' " The Bishop said, "I stood with my mouth open in astonishment. I didn't quite agree with his practical theology, but his surrender to God was perfect. All that he had he gave. It reminds me of what Jesus said about the woman who bathed his feet with ointment, 'She hath done what she could.' "

C. Roy Angell, *The Price Tags of Life* (Nashville: Broadman Press, 1959), pp. 7-9. Reprinted by permission of the publisher.

## ALL CHURCH MEMBERS TITHE—ONE WAY OR ANOTHER

I thought of what Warren Huyck said when I asked him how many tithers were in his church, and he answered, "Nineteen hundred." That startled me, and I asked him how many members there were, and he said, "Nineteen hundred." I exclaimed, "How in the world did you ever get them all to tithe?"

His answer is a classic. "Only about one hundred bring their tithes to the church. God collects it from the rest of them." And he added, "I mean it, Dr. Angell. God collects it from the rest of them."

C. Roy Angell, *Baskets of Silver* (Nashville: Broadman Press, 1955), p. 137. Reprinted by permission of the publisher.

## HOBSON'S CHOICE IN STEWARDSHIP

In the seventeenth century Thomas Hobson rented horses at Cambridge, England. He had a rule that any person who rented a horse must take the one standing nearest the stable door.

No matter what station in life the customer held, nor how much he might argue or wheedle, Hobson stuck to his rule.

It did not take long for "Hobson's choice," which was really no choice at all, to become a rather familiar statement and to pass into colloquial usage.

You know, when it comes to the matter of Christian stewardship Hobson's choice is what we have. We are all stewards. If we are Christian, then we are Christian stewards.

We don't have any decision to make as to *whether* we shall be stewards. Our decision is to *what kind* of stewards we will be. We can be good stewards by acknowledging God as the source of all our blessings and returning for His use a portion of the material blessing. Or we can be bad stewards and refuse to part with anything thinking it is all ours. In between the "good" and the "bad" of stewardship are all kinds of degrees of stewardship.

A steward is basically one who handles the affairs of another. When we begin with the basic understanding that it is God from whom all blessings flow then we shall try to serve and honor Him here below.

When it comes to stewardship all we have is Hobson's choice. We are already stewards. From this point we decide what kind of stewards we are.

JEC

## TO WHOM HAVE YOU MADE A SACRIFICE?

A news article in the New Orleans *Times-Picayune* of April

15, 1969, told of three men in India who had sacrificed a fifty-year-old man to a Hindu goddess in the belief that it would lead them to buried treasure.

This is not the only man in recent years who has been sacrificed for a fortune!

Many men have sacrificed themselves for material gain. Others have sacrificed a potentially productive life for society for a financially productive life. Some have sacrificed standards and principles for money. There have been those who have sacrificed meaningful family life and have thus sacrificed their family for a profit.

But is this the sacrifice God intended for us to make?

The New Testament talks about a sacrifice too. In Romans 12:1-2 this statement is found: "So then, my brothers, because of God's many mercies to us, I make this appeal to you: Offer yourselves as a living sacrifice to God, dedicated to his service and pleasing to him. This is the true worship that you should offer. Do not conform outwardly to the standards of this world, but let God transform you inwardly by a complete change of your mind. Then you will be able to know the will of God— what is good, and is pleasing to him, and is perfect" (TEV).

This is the sacrifice we ought to make: not a ritual sacrifice for fortune but a living sacrifice for service. With this kind of sacrifice we can know God's will and we can serve Christ's cause.

To whom have you made a sacrifice lately? To something that will not last? Or to God whose will is life?

JEC

## HOW GOD LOSES NICKELS

Gerald Kennedy, the Methodist bishop of Los Angeles, tells a story about a little boy whose mother gave him two nickels one Sunday morning and told him that one was to go into the Sunday school offering and the other was to spend as he pleased. Walking down the street and feeling very affluent, he was tossing one of the coins into the air when he dropped it. The coin rolled off the gutter into a drain and was lost. The boy looked very sad for a moment, and then he brightened up and said, "Well, Lord, I lost Your nickel."

God loses a lot of nickels that way!

Many people give God only what is left over after they have spent as they pleased. They expect the Lord to suffer the main losses.

If the tithe is the Lord's as the Bible says, and I believe it is, then the Lord's nickels have been spent on a lot that is not the Lord's business. The Lord loses a lot of nickels that way.

Many of the Lord's nickels were spent at the State Fair, at places of amusement, and at restaurants.

Some of the Lord's nickels are spent on vacations, week-end trips, and hunting expeditions.

There have been times when the Lord's money has gone for food, clothing, automobiles, and appliances.

If whenever a part of the money is lost or wasted or spent we have to say, "Well, Lord, there goes Your nickel," it explains how God loses nickels.

JEC

## DEPENDENCE ON GOD TO MEET NEED

One of the best illustrations of the kind of faith we ought to have was an experience that I had at Paisano. Dr. George W. Truett was on the other side of the world one summer, and I was preaching in his place at the Paisano Encampment in Texas. They had a unique custom of charging no one for meals throughout the ten days of that assembly. The meals were cooked in big, ranch chuck wagons and served cafeteria style.

On the last Sunday they took up an offering at the morning service for the next year. For twenty-five years Dr. Truett had taken this offering; and, of course, nobody could take an offering like Dr. Truett. The offerings had always been sufficient to finance the next year's encampment. On Saturday, a group of us, who had charge of the program for the year, met Brother Mike Milligan, God's missionary to the cowboys, whose vision and labor had established this encampment. Since I was preaching in Dr. Truett's place, they assigned me this tremendous task.

My faith wasn't strong enough to think I could do it like it ought to be done.

Saturday night came, and I prayed and wept a little as I asked God to please give me some extra help on the morrow. Early the next morning, I went over to see Brother Milligan. Paisano Encampment had been his dream, and he and God had brought it to pass. A thousand acres of land and a herd of cattle had been donated by the ranchers.

Mr. Milligan was growing old and getting very feeble. He had a long white beard and looked like the picture I have always had of Moses. He always sat down close to the pulpit in a chair covered with calfskin. Since he was losing his hearing, he cupped his hands behind his ears when I preached. His faith was as strong as the Rock of Gibraltar.

I sat down in front of him that morning and said, "Brother Milligan, all of us are deeply concerned about the offering today. The others have asked me to take it, but I think you ought to take it. These people will do anything you want them to do. They all love you, and everybody knows the great sacrifices you have made to preach the gospel of Jesus Christ to the cowboys."

He asked with a smile, "Are you afraid?"

And I said, "Yes, sir, we are all afraid."

Still smiling he said, "Stop worrying. This is God's work, and he will take care of it. Last night I got down on my knees, and I told God, 'You know Dr. Truett is not here, and you know you have only a few wonderful servants like Dr. Truett. Now, help Roy Angell tomorrow morning to take that offering."

He continued, "Before I got my clothes on this morning, there came a knock at the door. I opened it, and Mr. Kokernot [the wealthiest ranch owner there and a deacon in the First Baptist Church of San Antonio, beloved by all of us] was standing there with a check in his hand. He told me that he had just received a message from his ranch and that he would have to leave immediately. He handed me a check for one thousand dollars to put into the offering, and then he said, 'We want to send Dr. Truett a cablegram and tell him we have more than enough money in the bank for the next assembly. So here is a blank check with my name signed to it. When you count the offering, fill in the amount that we need so we can send him the message that the offering was more than sufficient."

C. Roy Angell, *God's Gold Mines* (Nashville: Broadman Press, 1962), pp. 64-65. Reprinted by permission of the publisher.

## A RULE FOR LIFE: GIVE ALL YOU CAN

John Wesley's rule of life was to *save* all he could and *give* all he could. When he was at Oxford he had an income of 30 pounds a year. He lived on 28 pounds and gave 2 pounds away. When his income increased to 60 pounds, 90 pounds and 120 pounds a year, he still lived on 28 pounds and gave the balance away. The Accountant-General for Household Plate demanded a return from him. His reply was, "I have two silver tea spoons at London and two at Bristol. This is all the plate which I have at present; and I shall not buy any more, while so many around me want bread."

From *The Gospel of Luke,* translated and interpreted by William Barclay. Published in the U.S.A. by The Westminster Press, 1957. p. 168. Used by permission.

## GIVING TO RIVAL ANOTHER PERSON

In her book, *A Goodly Heritage,* Mary Ellen Chase has a delightful chapter where she writes of her girlhood experience on Sunday mornings in a New England Congregational church. She recalls those features of worship that usually amuse children, and the offering was always one of them. It seems that her grandmother gave a substantial lump sum to the church every year and, since everybody knew about it, she made it a rule to place no offering on the collection plate. Another well-to-do parishioner, Mrs. Harriet Morton, contributed an equal sum by cheque and also let the plate pass by. Then, to grandmother's distress, her rival in good works suddenly began making additional offerings by depositing a coin in the plate each Sunday. The size of the coin varied. Not to be outdone, grandmother determined to contribute a similar amount, no more and no less. By a system of hand signals one of the grand-children sitting behind Mrs. Morton let grandmother know what her rival had put on the plate, but one Sunday grand-mother, who was becoming increasingly short-sighted and deaf, whispered in a voice audible to the whole congregation, "How much did Hattie Morton give this morning?" Mary Ellen Chase writes, "I regret to say that neither her voice nor her intonation was strictly in keeping with the ideal atmosphere of a Christian edifice."

Mary Ellen Chase, *A Goodly Heritage* (Henry Holt and Co., Inc., 1932), cited by Leonard Griffith, *This Is Living* (Nashville: Abingdon Press, 1966), pp. 154-155. Reprinted by permission of the publisher.

# ... CONCERNING WHEN TO GIVE

## WHEN TO START TITHING

Dr. A. J. Gordon gives the following story about William Colgate: "Many years ago a lad of sixteen left home to seek his fortune. All his worldly possessions were tied up in a bundle which he carried in his hand. As he trudged along he met an old neighbor, the captain of a canalboat, and the following conversation took place, which changed the whole current of the boy's life:

" 'Well, William, where are you going?'

" 'I don't know,' he answered. 'Father is too poor to keep me at home any longer, and says I must make a living for myself now.'

" 'There is no trouble about that,' said the captain. 'Be sure you start right and you will get along finely.'

"William told his friend that the only trade he knew anything about was soap and candle-making, at which he had helped his father while at home.

" 'Well,' said the old man, 'let me pray with you once more and give you a little advice, and then I will let you go.'

"They both kneeled down upon the tow-path; the dear old man prayed earnestly for William and then gave him this advice, 'Someone will soon be the leading soapmaker in New York. It can be you as well as anyone. I hope it may. Be a good man; give your heart to Christ; give the Lord all that belongs to Him of every dollar you earn; make an honest soap; give a full pound, and I am certain you will yet be a prosperous and rich man.'

"When the boy arrived in the city, he found it hard to get work. Lonesome and far from home he remembered his mother's words and the last words of the canalboat captain. He was then led to 'seek first the Kingdom of God and His righteousness,' and united with the church. He remembered his promise to the old captain, and the first dollar he earned brought up the question of the Lord's part. In the Bible he found that the Jews were commanded to give one-tenth; so he said, 'If the Lord will take one-tenth, I will give that.' And so he did; and ten cents of every dollar was sacred to the Lord. He prospered; his business grew; his family was blessed; his soap sold; and he grew rich faster than he had ever hoped. He then gave the Lord two-tenths and prospered more than ever; then he gave three-tenths, then four-tenths; then five-tenths. He educated his family, settled all his plans for life, and thereafter gave the whole of his income to the Lord."

Reprinted from "The Reflector," the bulletin of the First Baptist Church of Jonesboro, Louisiana.


## A BOY'S DECISION TO TITHE

Recently I spoke at a loyalty banquet in one of the big cities of Louisiana. The dinner was arranged as a part of the financial program of the church, and the emphasis was on tithing. To me the most thrilling part of that program was the testimony given by a Christian layman. When he was introduced, the applause was thunderous. He was good to look at. He had iron-gray hair. Gentleness, kindness, and happiness were written all over his face. As the applause kept on, he just stood quietly and smiled and by-and-by lifted his hand in recognition of the tribute. This is about what he said: "When I was a boy of fourteen, I came home one Saturday with my first pay envelope. I didn't open it till I got home. Mother and I sat down at the kitchen table, and I poured the money out. There was thirteen one dollar bills and twenty cents. I thought it was the biggest pile of money I had ever seen. My mother said, 'What are you going to do with it, Son?' I told her, 'I am going to buy a pair of skates with some of it, and I am going to buy a pair of gloves. Then I want to buy you something, Mother,' 'What will you do with the balance of it?' she asked. I told her I thought I would start a savings account. Then, quietly smiling, she said, 'Aren't you going to give God a tithe of it?' 'Do I have to?' was my quick response. After a moment of silence she said:

'No, Son, it is your money, and you don't have to give God any of it, but your father and I tithe. We get a lot of pleasure out of it, and I am sure that our tithing has had much to do with the kind of a home that you have. Suppose you go up to your room and think about it, and I would suggest you pray about it, then make your own decision.'

"I stayed upstairs a couple of hours. When I came down, I went straight to Mother and asked her if she would answer a question for me. She said, 'Certainly, what is it?' 'Suppose I don't tithe. Suppose I don't give God any of it. What would happen to me?' She looked at me and soberly said, 'Nothing, Son, nothing now.' I was greatly relieved and stood there a moment before resuming the conversation. 'Mamma, what will happen if I do tithe?' Her face was beaming as she answered: 'That's what I wanted you to ask me. The same thing that's happened to your daddy and me. You will find more peace of mind, more joy, more satisfaction in being a good steward than in any one thing you will ever do. The whole world will be sweeter to you; you will love to say your prayers; you will be proud of your religion; and you will know that God is proud of you. You will grow strong spiritually. Your Christianity and your church will be very precious to you.'"

The speaker stood there a bit choked up, and the eight hundred people in front of him had their emotions deeply stirred. When he could talk again, he said in a husky voice: "You know, it makes me tremble, tremble, tremble, like that old song says, when I think, 'Suppose I hadn't started to tithe?' Out of the bottom of my heart I can say that nothing in the world has meant as much to me as my relationship to my Heavenly Father, and I doubt if I would ever have enjoyed this relationship if I hadn't started tithing."

C. Roy Angell, *The Price Tags of Life* (Nashville: Broadman Press, 1959), pp. 56-57. Used by permission.

## REMEMBER GOD IN SUCCESS, TOO

Dr. W. D. Nowlin, one of the veteran preachers of Florida, told me an incident from his life which splendidly illustrates this. He said, "A fine young man, whose name was John, was superintendent of the Sunday school in one of my churches. He had the esteem and confidence of the whole town, and when he opened his own business, it prospered immediately. John was a splendid Christian and never missed a service. He was active in every department of the church. He was a consistent tither and one of the most faithful Christians in the church.

"His business succeeded so that he moved into larger quarters, and at the end of the second year he opened a branch store in the next town. In the meantime, his tithe grew until he was by far the largest giver in the church. At the end of four years he had opened six branch stores, and his tithe had grown to $100 a week, but there his contribution stopped. Along there somewhere he asked to be relieved of the superintendency of the Sunday school until he could get his business organized better. He also stopped coming to prayer meeting, and then we began to miss him at church on Sunday. When I went to see him, he told me that his business demanded so much of his time that often he spent week ends in one of the other towns getting things organized and straightened out. Though his income grew larger, his contributions stayed at $100 a week.

"One day I went down to his office. I closed the door behind me as I went in. I said to him, 'John, I'm worried about you. You are missing church and apparently you are losing interest in the kingdom's work, and I am afraid you are not giving your tithe to the Lord any longer.'

"He said, 'Brother Nowlin, my tithe is too big, and I thought a hundred dollars a week was enough to give to the Lord's work. My business is so big I don't have as much time as I used to have.'

"I said, 'John,' will you get down here on your knees and pray with me?'

"After we knelt, I began the prayer like this: 'Dear Lord, you have prospered John too much. You have given him too much business and too much success, and his tithe is too big to give to you, so dear Lord, please for John's sake and for the kingdom's work, burn down some of his stores. Let some of them fail; take some of the business away from him so he can be the same John we used to love and who used to work so faithfully for you.'

"I felt John tremble a little, and then he spoke out, 'Mr. Nowlin, let me take up from there.' His prayer was one that came from a contrite and humble heart. He asked God's forgiveness. He promised he would do it differently from now on. John came back and took his place as superintendent again and became once more the leading spirit in our church."

C. Roy Angell, *Baskets of Silver* (Nashville: Broadman Press, 1955), pp. 113-115. Used by permission.


## START LIFE WITH CHRIST BY TITHING: A MODERN RICH YOUNG RULER

Some years ago there came to see me a man I could characterize as Madison Avenue at its most ultra-ultra. Only he wasn't from Madison Avenue, but from Chicago, where I believe the corresponding symbol of smart sophistication is La Salle Street. This man was meticulously dressed. He obviously had a tailor who knew his business. He had a cane too and he knew how to carry it. He laid his cane and gloves and hat down on my desk as he sat down with me. There had never been cane, hat and gloves on my desk before and I thought to myself that now I had arrived! The man said to me, "I want to tell you something, Dr. Peale. I never did go to church until recently. I was born near Chicago, on the North Shore. My family was well fixed. We've always been well off since my grandfather made the money. We were part of the so-called upper crust. But I began to feel nervous, unhappy, disconsolate. Somebody gave me one of your books and I read it, read it two or three times, made a list of all the things you said to do and then set out to do them. I believed in your ideas and did my best to put them into practice. You claim that if a person does these things he will have peace, happiness and contentment. I must tell you that I did get some benefit, but I haven't got enough and I'm not very happy."

"What church do you go to?" I asked.

"Well, I don't go to any regularly. I only go to church

now and then," he replied. "I'm looking around in Chicago for a preacher I like."

"How much do you give to the church?" I asked.

"Give?" he repeated. "I don't give anything."

"But I suppose you're a big giver to the Community Chest in Chicago?"

He shook his head. "I don't give them any more than I have to."

"You don't believe in giving, eh?"

"Well," he admitted, "I just give what I have to."

But, you know, I liked this man. He was earnest. He was after something. So I said, "Well, I'll tell you, Jesus makes it very clear that a man has to pick up a cross. Have you ever carried a cross?"

He looked at me in a puzzled way and said, "No, I can't claim that."

"The people who carry the cross for Jesus Christ get wonderful blessings of happiness because they are doing something for mankind," I continued. "Now I am sure you're just the kind of fellow Jesus wants. I am sure He's got His finger on you. He is agitating you and making you miserable because He wants you. And if you come through you'll have a wonderful life."

"Well," he asked, "what do I do first?"

You should tithe," I answered. "That would be a good place to start."

"What is that?"

I explained to him that the Bible says you are supposed to give the Lord one tenth of everything you receive.

"Boy!" he exclaimed, "that's the biggest percentage I ever heard of. Ten percent?"

Ignoring his pained surprise, I asked, "What are you doing these days?"

"My wife and I are taking a little trip around the world."

"How much do you think that will cost you?"

"With the tickets and what my wife buys," he said, "I'll be lucky if it costs me less than ten thousand dollars."

"What's one tenth of ten thousand?" I asked him.

"One thousand."

"That's right. I would suggest you get out a check and since you don't belong to any other church write a check to the Marble Collegiate Church for one thousand dollars. That will start you tithing."

Well, he said he would think it over. And as he walked out I had to practice a lot of positive thinking to believe I'd ever see him again. But I received a letter from him mailed at London. He and his wife had crossed by ship, had been five days on the water. "I had the most miserable crossing," he wrote, "but here's your check." When this man got back to Chicago he joined a church and became one of its most active members. I had advised him to tithe his time as well as his money. He went to the minister and said, "You can have ten percent of my time. I'll do anything you want me to do." He also made a list of people to pray for. He went all out. And the peace and power and love of God engulfed him. Some time later he remarked to me, "Isn't it wonderful how joyous life is when you live with Jesus in your thinking?"

Norman Vincent Peale, "God Will Help You If You Let Him" (Pawling, N.Y.: Foundation for Christian Living, 1963), XIV, 8, pp. 10-12. Reprinted by permission of the publisher.

# ... CONCERNING ATTITUDES TOWARD GIVING

## BOTH GLAD AND SAD

An old legend relates that one night long ago three horsemen were riding across a desert. As they crossed the dry bed of a river, a voice called out in the darkness, "Halt!" They obeyed. The voice then told them to dismount, pick up a handful of pebbles, put the pebbles in their pockets, and remount. The voice then said, "You have done as I commanded. Tomorrow at sun-up you will be both glad and sorry." The horsemen rode on pondering the meaning of this experience. When the sun rose the following morning they reached into their pockets and found that a miracle had happened. The pebbles had been transformed into precious stones—diamonds, rubies and so on. Then they remembered the warning. *They were both glad and sorry— glad they had taken some—and sorry they had not taken more.*

"Remember the words of the Lord Jesus, how He said, It is more blessed to give than receive."

Kenneth Mills in "The Visitor," the bulletin of the Haynes Avenue Baptist Church, Shreveport, Louisiana.

## INCREDIBLE, I CALL IT!

A man took his family into a restaurant. They sat down at a clean table, ordered a sumptuous meal, ate with satisfaction and delight. When the waitress brought the check, the man said, "Oh, I don't believe in paying for meals. Please give the check to that man over there. He will probably be glad to pay it." The waitress took the check to the man at a nearby table. The man accepted the check and paid for it, even leaving a tip for the waitress. Incredible, I call it!

A woman went to the supermarket where all manner of goodies which characterize American eating were spread out in long rows. She filled her cart with everything from a case of ginger-ale to a prime roast of beef and a large bag of out-of-season fruit. When she came to the check-out desk the cashier rang up the bill and said, "$35.60, please." The woman put on a horrified look and said, "But I'm going to take a trip to Europe next week and I just don't have the money to pay for this food. I'll just let these folks behind me in line pay for it." And behold, the folks in line behind reached for their pocketbooks and pulled out the money and paid the bill. Incredible!

A family lived in Pleasantville, one of the nicest towns in the world. The children attended fine schools, the family enjoyed the paved streets, and the excellent water and sewage facilities, the public works and the community hospital. They liked this town. But one day a tax bill arrived and they frowned and tore it up, and threw it away. Some time later a tax collector knocked at their door and announced himself. "Get away from here," shouted the father, "that's the trouble with this town, always asking for money. I don't believe in paying taxes. Let my neighbors pay it if they want to." And the neighbors liked these people and they got together and paid their taxes! Incredible!

NOW THERE WAS A FAMILY THAT BELONGED TO A WONDERFUL CHURCH . . . Sorry, just can't bear to tell this story . . . you tell it yourself. It is utterly incredible. And it's true!

Reprinted from "The Messenger" of the First Baptist Church, Zachary, Louisiana.

## REAL LOVE IN ACTION

Back in the dim, hard days of the depression, author John Steinbeck went to Hollywood, a place he did not like. The false glitter and glamor of the place, the false values, irritated him.

He was not in need of Hollywood's fat pay checks; he had just published his famous novel, *Grapes of Wrath,* in which he depicted so strongly the plight of the poverty-stricken victims of that depression. But he went, and wrote the film version or scenario of *Grapes of Wrath* for the movie producers.

He was paid $6,000 for six weeks' work—and he promptly gave three thousand migrant workers $2.00 apiece. He was close to these people—too close to merely write a book about them and then forget them. What he did was love in action.

Reprinted from *Tarbell's Teacher's Guide.*

## A POSITIVE PURPOSE

When Colonel Lindbergh landed in Paris from his first trans-Atlantic flight, his associates here sent him the offer of a contract for a million dolars. His brief, explicit, return cable is worthy of a place among the undying utterances of this generation. "You must remember," he said, "this expedition was not organized to make money but to advance aviation."

Harry Emerson Fosdick, *The Power to See It Through* (New York: Harper and Brothers, 1935), p. 69. Reprinted by permission of the publisher.

## EVERYONE DOES NOT WORSHIP MONEY

Said Voltaire, "When it is a question of money, everybody is of the same religion." That is a lie! When it is a question of money all men are not of the same religion. John Milton gave his life to a cause, spent his sight on it, and for writing *Paradise Lost* received ten pounds. Beethoven made a disappointing pittance out of his performance of the immortal Ninth Symphony. Such men cared first for things creative, beautiful, not for sale. Spinoza, the philosopher, lived in Holland and humbly made a poor livelihood polishing lenses, meanwhile thinking great thoughts about God. Louis XIV offered him a pension and patronage if he would dedicate only one book to his majesty. Spinoza did not believe in Louis XIV, so in poverty he polished lenses and thought great thoughts.

Harry Emerson Fosdick, *What Is Vital in Religion* (New York: Harper and Bros., 1955), p. 175. Reprinted by permission of the publisher.

## LOVE OF MONEY SHUTS OUT THE FACE OF GOD

The English preacher, Robert Hall, tells of a man who

came to criticize a statement he made in a sermon. The preacher immediately recognized that the man was in love with money. He opened his Bible at random and pointed to the word "God." "Can you see that?" he asked his visitor. "Of course," replied the man. The preacher took a half sovereign and placed it over the word. "Can you see it now?" he asked. Material values must never be placed ahead of spiritual values, unless one wishes his life to become a tragedy.

Fred M. Wood, *Bible Truth in Person* (Nashville: Broadman Press, 1965), p. 83. Reprinted by permission of the author.

## REFUSAL TO BE ENSLAVED BY MONEY

George Truett tells of a wealthy broker who had a ship lost at sea containing $40,000 worth of goods. He was at the point of nervous frustration because of the anticipated loss. Suddenly he realized he was a slave to money, and he immediately sat down and wrote a check for the same amount to a benevolent cause in town. This man would not be enslaved by materialism.

Fred M. Wood, *Bible Truth in Person* (Nashville: Broadman Press, 1965), p. 85. Reprinted by permission of the author.

## MONEY CAN BE DEADLY

In one of McGuffey's readers there is a story of a miser who had under his basement a subbasement that was known only to himself. Here he kept his silver and gold. Here he would come secretly to worship. It was his custom to run his bony fingers through the coins and listen to the music of their clank, as he said, "O my Beauties, O my Beauties!" But one day, while he was thus worshiping, a vagrant wind blew the door of the subbasement shut. It fastened with a spring lock that could only be turned from the outside. Thus the miser was shut in with his gold. Years later, when men tore down his old house, they found a skeleton draped over a heap of coins. He had taken money and made it is god, and that god had destroyed him. But money was no more deadly for him than it is for those who, today, change it from a means into an end.

Clovis G. Chappell, *Ten Rules for Living* (New York and Nashville: Abingdon Press, 1938), p. 34. Reprinted by permission of the publisher.

## UNDISCOVERED WEALTH: A GOLD MINE IN THE ATTIC

In one of our daily papers there was a news item with this caption over it, "Is there a gold mine in your attic?" The story beneath was very fascinating. It read about like this. An elderly woman was poking around in her attic in search of something she needed. In an old bureau drawer she found a faded, yellow envelope containing some valuable-looking documents. She looked at them for awhile and then decided she would take them to the bank to see if they were worth anything. She showed them to a teller and told him where she found them. It took him only a moment to say, "They may be *very* valuable; please wait just a minute."

He took them to an executive of the bank, who immediately came back with him to the window and invited the lady to come into his private office. You can imagine her astonishment when he told her they were bonds worth approximately $60,000 on the current market. He offered to sell them for her immediately if she needed the money. The writer of the article ended the story with this: "There may not be a gold mine in the attic of your home, but as Russell Conwell once said, 'There are acres of diamonds all around you that have not been discovered. Some of them may be in your mind and personality.' "

C. Roy Angell, *God's Gold Mines* (Nashville: Broadman Press, 1962), p. 1. Used by permission.

## THE DIFFERENCE BETWEEN MAKING A LIVING AND MAKING A LIFE

In 1923, nine of the world's wealthiest men met in the Edgewater Beach Hotel in Chicago. Twenty-five years later their lives tell a tragic story.

Charles Schwab, president of the world's largest independent steel company died in bankruptcy, living on borrowed money the last five years of his life.

Samuel Insull, president of the world's largest utility company, died in a foreign land—penniless and a fugitive from justice.

Howard Hopson, president of the world's largest gas company, went insane.

Arthur Cutten, leading speculator in wheat, died abroad and insolvent.

Richard Whitney, president of the New York Stock Exchange, a few years ago was released from Sing Sing.

Albert Fall, a member of the President's cabinet, was pardoned from prison so that he might die at home.

Jesse Livermore, the greatest "bear" on Wall Street, committed suicide.

Ivan Krueger, head of the world's greatest monopoly, also died a suicide.

Leon Fraser, president of the Bank of International Settlements, died a suicide.

Of them all someone said, "All of these men learned well the art of money-making, but not one of them learned how to live."

Herschel H. Hobbs, *Studying Life and Work Lessons,* July, August, September, 1969 (Nashville: Convention Press, 1969), pp. 55-56. Used by permission.

# ... CONCERNING THE EFFECT OF GIVING

## A TURNING POINT IN ECONOMIC LIFE

Our gifts to God never make us poorer, because God, the Author of all that we possess, continually replenishes the resources that we want to use for His work. This truth was pressed upon me one evening by a very fine Christian, successful in business and loyal to the Church. I sat in his luxurious home chatting with him and his wife and remarked how fortunate they were in their material affluence. Quickly he broke in and said, "It hasn't always been like this. During the economic depression I was more than once out of a job. Sometimes we didn't even know where the next meal was coming from. We really struck rock-bottom before the tide turned." "When did it turn?" I asked him. He looked at his wife, as though they shared a secret, then he said, "I honestly believe that our circumstances began to change on the day when we made up our minds that, whatever God gave us, no matter how small, we would give back a tenth of it to Him." "Have you stuck by that decision?" I asked. "Always," he replied, "and always I have found that the more I give to God, the more God gives me to give back to Him."

Leonard Griffith, *This Is Living* (Nashville: Abingdon Press, 1966), pp. 157-158. Reprinted by permission of the publisher.

## A PARTNERSHIP IN CHRISTIAN SERVICE

It was a memorable event in the life of our congregation when we welcomed home two of our distinguished members who serve as medical superintendents of mission hospitals in South India. They told us shocking stories of people living in the most primitive conditions and of the unceasing battle to treat illnesses caused only by malnutrition and lack of sanitation. Yet they spoke hopefully as they recalled killer-diseases which have been conquered during their own lifetime and they spoke gratefully of our gifts which make possible the prosecution of this war. They told us that, with the money we gave them on their last furlough, one had bought a new operating-table and the other an anaesthetic machine, and they said that through these gifts we stand beside the surgeons and nurses every time a patient undergoes surgery. Here were these men, magnificent servants of Christ, dedicating their skills and very lives to His compassionate ministry of healing, and we were their partners in God's great enterprise. In that partnership we felt a sense of privilege far out of proportion to our small investment.

Leonard Griffith, *This Is Living* (Nashville: Abingdon Press, 1966), pp. 153-154. Reprinted by permission of the publisher.

## AN UNUSED ENVELOPE TALKS

Look inside this year's church envelope box. If you see me there, I'll tell you a story . . .

I'll tell you the Sunday you missed church. Just check the date written on me. I can't tell you why you missed. You'll have to think back to remember. Was it a good reason—a good reason, not an excuse!

I was designed to hold any amount you want to give. I look much better made fat with a love offering than I do flat, unsealed, and useless. I have no power over myself. I am your servant. I had counted so much on going to the Lord's treasury on my day . . .

I can tell you about your spiritual life, too. When I am used I speak of an honest heart. I could have been filled and taken to church later even though you missed attending on my Sunday.

Because I am still unused I speak of limits placed on God's work. Do you hear the cry of children without parents, do you see the sick without care, the ignorant untaught, the church not built, the Bibles not sent, the gospel not preached, the lost without hope?

I could have helped meet these needs if I had been used. I wanted to. You didn't fail me, you failed God; but you did make me share in the misery of the world.

I am empty and heartbroken. Look at me! Let me touch your conscience and stir your heart!

> Truthfully,
> *Your Unused Envelope*

Reprinted from "Church Chimes," the church bulletin of the First Baptist Church, Shreveport, Louisiana.

## TITHIN' EGGS!

Once there was a lady who put up a sign by her farm house which read:

HEN EGGS .......... 35¢ A DOZEN
TITHIN' EGGS ...... 45¢ A DOZEN

Travelers were often curious about the sign so they stopped to buy from the woman. When they asked her to explain, she would bring out two baskets of eggs. She would point to one basket and say, "These are hen eggs." Then she pointed to the other basket and announced, "These are tithin' eggs."

"See the difference?" she would ask. "The tithin' eggs are larger. I have been tithing to my church for a long time. Every day when I gather the eggs in, I place them in groups of ten. Then I pick the largest egg from each group and put it in my tithin' basket. I sell these for the extra price so that I'm not only tithing my income but I'm making some extra money for my Lord."

Reprinted from "The Queebach Herald" of the Queensboro Baptist Church, Shreveport, Louisiana.

## A MODERN PARABLE

The treasurer of a congregation resigned. The church asked another to take his position, a man who managed the local grain elevator. He agreed under two conditions:

1. That no report be necessary for one whole year.
2. That no one ask him any questions during this one year period.

The church gulped, but finally agreed, since he was a trusted man in the community, and well known, because most of them did business with him as manager of the local elevator.

At the end of the year he gave this report:

> The indebtedness of $25,000 on the church was paid.
> The minister's salary had been increased.
> The mission quota was paid 200%.
> There were no outstanding bills, and there was a cash balance of $12,000.

Immediately a shocked congregation asked, "How come?" Quietly he answered, "Most of you bring your grain to my elevator. As you did business with me I simply withheld 10% on your behalf and gave it to the church in your name. You never missed it. Do you see what we could do for the Lord if we were willing to give the first tithe to God, who really owns it?"

Reprinted from the bulletin of the University Baptist Church, Baton Rouge, Louisiana.

## LIVING AFTER DEATH THROUGH STEWARDSHIP

H. E. Briggs of Ponca City was a strong believer in Christian stewardship, and he proved it—both in life and in death. He was an active supporter of the stewardship emphasis in First Church there each year, including budget campaigns, pledge cards and tithing solicitation. For many years he was an active deacon and trustee of the church, serving as chairman of the deacons over a long period.

His son, Philip H. Briggs, professor of religious education and church administration at Midwestern Seminary, Kansas City, Mo., was called home from a speaking engagement at Ridgecrest Assembly in 1963 because of his father's death. The son tells it this way: "After the funeral, Mother said that she wanted me to have Daddy's billfold. Inside it were two signed envelopes with the next two Sunday's tithe. The next Sunday while still in Ponca City I turned these envelopes in to my father's Sunday school department where he served as associate superintendent.

I knew he would have wanted that had he known! Though dead a week, in this act he was still quite alive."

*The Baptist Messenger,* October 5, 1967. Reprinted by permission of the publisher.

## SOME OF GOD'S BLESSINGS ARE MATERIAL BLESSINGS

One day I was speaking in a former pastorate on "The Unsearchable Riches of God," and I made the statement that these riches of which Paul spoke were not material riches but spiritual riches. After the sermon a lawyer friend of twenty years' standing came up and put a hand on each of my shoulders. He put his face up close to mine and said: "Roy, don't ever make the mistake again. Don't ever say that God doesn't pour out upon us material riches when we prove our good stewardship. Come down to my office in the morning. I have something to show you." The next morning I walked into one of the finest suites of offices I ever saw. It was elegantly appointed and furnished. He escorted me through the ten or twelve rooms and introduced me to his associates and partners. When we came back to his private office, he asked: "Do you remember what my office was like when you left here? Do you remember that it consisted of one shabby room, no carpet on the floor, and an old battered desk? I did not even have a secretary. Many times I have said to others, and I say it now to you: 'God gave me this prosperity. God made me immensely wealthy. God did it, and if you want to look at my books, you will see that I don't give a tenth—I give him one half.' So I repeat what I said last night, 'Don't ever say that God's riches are confined to spiritual things.'" So I say here with assurance, God *is* rich in material things.

C. Roy Angell, *The Price Tags of Life* (Nashville: Broadman Press, 1959), pp. 90-91. Used by permission.

## YOUR LIFE IS WHAT YOU MAKE IT

A successful businessman related the following incident:
"I had an appointment at 7:00 P.M. with one of the big industrialists of our city. I arrived at his home a little before

seven and was ushered into a beautifully appointed living room. I sat down gingerly in a big chair. The room was so immaculately clean and furnished in such excellent taste that I felt a little out of place. While I waited for the man to finish his dinner, I looked down at my clothes and wished I had shined my shoes and shaved and cleaned up a little. I could hear laughter from the dining room, and I sat there thinking, 'I have missed something by being a bachelor and not having a bunch of children and a nice home of my own.'

"My thoughts were interrupted by a five-year-old boy who came dashing from the dining room. He stopped directly in front of me and without a word, looked me over and then said, 'My daddy told me that you were a millionaire. Is that true?'

"I smiled at him and nodded. 'Yes, I guess that's true.'

" 'He said that you are a self-made man, too. Are you?'

" 'Yes, son, I guess I am a self-made man.'

"Once more he looked me over from my dusty shoes to my unkempt hair and then stared me full in the face and said innocently, 'What did you make yourself like that for?' Without waiting for an answer, he bounded out of the room.

"I felt my face turn crimson, and once more I looked with embarrassment at the baggy knees of my trousers and at a necktie that had spots on it; I knew my collar was not fresh and that I needed a haircut. After I had finished my appointment, I went home and took a good look at myself in the mirror. The examination made me very unhappy and led me to take a good look at my whole life. I thought of what the little boy couldn't see—the inside of me was as unkempt as the outside. I sat there in my room a long time and finally got my Bible and had a session with God."

He closed with this sentence: "I guess a man's life is what he makes it."

C. Roy Angell, *Baskets of Silver* (Nashville: Broadman Press, 1955), pp. 58-59. Used by permission.

## AN ACCOUNTANT'S TESTIMONY: TITHING FIRMS DON'T GO BANKRUPT

One of the best businessmen on the gold coast of Florida

told me recently that he had learned a startling fact from the accounting firm that audited his books each year. The representative said to him, "I am glad to see your firm tithes, and I am glad that you tithe personally, too." The businessman answered, "Thank you. I guess you are a tither yourself?"

After a moment he said very slowly, "No, I never got around to it, but I ought to, because I have been auditing books in Miami for more than twenty years, and I have never seen a firm that tithes go bankrupt or even get in serious trouble." My friend said, "Say that over again, for it interests me deeply." The auditor took his glasses off and talked for ten minutes naming some of the finest business firms in Florida who were tithers.

C. Roy Angell, *Baskets of Silver* (Nashville: Broadman Press, 1955), pp. 136-137. Used by permission.

## A TREASURE NO ONE CAN STEAL

But I read this story of another man, a college professor. He was rather a frail chap physically, but he had a clear mind and a clean heart. He was in love with a girl of great vigor and charm. He had a rival who was an athletic fellow, magnetic and attractive. This rival seemed to have everything that could appeal. Therefore, nobody was surprised when he became engaged to the girl of their choice. But he was lacking in character. In his eagerness for easy money, he stole certain trustfunds that were committed to his care. The circumstances were such that it became the duty of the professor to witness against him. And it was through this testimony that he was convicted and sent to serve a term in the penitentiary.

One dark night years later, when the rain was falling in torrents, the professor was alone in his library. Suddenly he felt a breath of cold wind. He looked up from his work, and there before him stood his rival in the garb of a convict with a revolver in his hand. "I have dreamed of this meeting for a long time," said the intruder bitterly. "You have ruined my life and now I am going to make you pay." "I did not ruin your life," the little professor answered quietly. "You ruined it for yourself when you became a thief. Nobody can ruin one's life

but one's self." "How I have suffered," the convict continued. "And how I have longed to make you suffer as I have
suffered!" "But that you cannot do," the professor replied. "You
can kill me, of course, but you are entirely powerless to make
me suffer as you have suffered. If you kill me, my suffering will
be physical only, and doubtless very brief. Death will be for
me the gateway into a fuller life. Therefore, you cannot make
me suffer as you have suffered." This man possessed a wealth
that thieves cannot break through and steal. No wonder the
convict stood awed in his presence. His foe had that which is
proof against any weapon that man can wield.

Clovis G. Chappell, *The Sermon on the Mount* (New York and
Nashville: Abingdon Press, 1930), pp. 189-190. Reprinted by permission
of the publisher.

## AS YOU GIVE YOU GAIN

Not long ago I had the privilege of addressing twelve
thousand students at Brigham Young University in Utah. That
university is under the auspices of the Mormon Church, and its
president is a dynamic man by the name of Ernest L. Wilkinson, formerly a lawyer. Mr. Wilkinson has written a little booklet
on tithing and we got to discussing the subject. He says, "I've
found that the way to unlock the flow of power is to give." The
Bible says, "Bring ye all the tithes into the storehouse . . . and
prove me now herewith, saith the Lord of hosts, if I will not
open you the windows of heaven, and pour you out a blessing,
that there shall not be room enough to receive it." Mr. Wilkinson maintains that the wise people are the people who believe
this and who practice this belief. And he tells about a man in
Grand Rapids who manufactured furniture.

This man, using the ordinary procedures of business, got
into difficulties and practically went broke. He was able to save
the factory, but his credit was very thin. The bankers wouldn't
loan him money. However, he had a few friends who out of
sentiment loaned him enough to get started again. But he said
to himself: "Somehow or other things elude me. I haven't got
what it takes to do a successful job. I'm failing at some point."

Then he began to pray and read the Bible and he got the idea of tithing—giving ten percent of your income and your time to the Lord. So when he was ready to start his factory up on a little, thin line of credit, he went to his office and knelt down and said to the Lord, "Lord, this plant, such as it is, is Yours. I accept You now as my Partner and I will give the first ten percent all the rest of my life to You."

He began to make furniture again and he kept giving a part of his money away and as he gave, more money came back to him. Then his credit got better because his results were better and the bankers began to loan him money. They were puzzled because part of the money they loaned him he used in his business, but part of it he gave away. They said, "That isn't practical." But his business grew and he brought blessings to other people.

As you give you gain, not only monetarily, but in all of the more precious blessings of life. The basic spiritual law of the universe, demonstrated by Jesus Christ who gave His life, is that blessings come from giving yourself away.

Norman Vincent Peale, "The Magic of Believing" (Pawling, N.Y.: Foundation for Christian Living, 1964), XV, 11, pp. 11-12. Reprinted by permission of the publisher.

## MY FATHER'S STEWARDSHIP TESTIMONY

My father died in 1965. For many years he had been a Baptist deacon as was his father before him.

My father took his Christian faith very seriously. Stewardship was an important part of Christianity to him. And to him stewardship meant tithing. No matter what else waited he made sure that the Lord received His tithe.

I don't know that I ever heard him put it in these words but I think my father would have said that he practiced tithing for three reasons: the Bible taught it; it was God's will; and it was right. This combination of reasons was convincing enough to him.

Tithing did not insure my father of a long life. He died at sixty-two years of age, which isn't a ripe old age these days.

Tithing did not make my father wealthy. At his death he did not leave a great deal of wealth, a lot of insurance, or vast land holdings. We always had food, clothing, and shelter, but our family was far from wealthy. Dad worked long, hard hours all his life.

Tithing did not keep bad things from happening to him either. We had our share of crises, things breaking down and such. My father died with cancer after eighteen months of suffering and several rounds of surgery.

If tithing did not make my father wealthy, insure him of a long life, or keep him from suffering, why did he tithe? Because he thought it was what he should do as a Christian. Since the Bible taught it, it was God's will, and it was right, Dad faithfully tithed.

By the way, part of the legacy my father left me was the memory and influence of a strong, practicing Christian faith—and a vital tithing testimony.

JEC

## HOLDING THE ROPES

The first society for the work of foreign missions was formed in 1792 in England. The society was born out of the missionary impulse of William Carey and his eloquent and insistent pleas that Baptists should do something for the conversion of the heathen. When the missionary society was formed after Carey's efforts he offered himself as the first missionary.

In 1791 he had published a little book entitled *An Inquiry into the Obligations of Christians to Use Means for the Conversion of the Heathen*. In 1792 he had preached his famous sermon based on Isaiah 54:2-3 at the Nottinghamshire Baptist Association. Then in October of 1792 at the home of a Widow Wallis the mission society was formed and the modern mission movement was begun. In offering himself as a missionary Carey said to the men, "I will go down into the well, if you will hold the ropes." By holding the ropes he meant if they would give him support.

This is what we are doing through Christian stewardship. We are holding the ropes for all the work that Christ is doing through the churches.

JEC

## CANNOT OUTGIVE GOD

A teen-age lad who was working hard to help support his family wanted very much to get a new winter suit of clothes as the other members of his Sunday school class had, but he had denied himself that privilege because of his loyalty to his family. Finally, the mother decided the time had come when the family should deny itself a bit in order that this son might have a new suit. Accordingly, she arranged to let him keep a whole week's wages with which to purchase the suit.

When the son went to church Sunday morning, however, he heard an eloquent appeal for foreign missions and decided to deny himself the suit in order that he might give the whole week's wages to missions. The next day when he reported for work he was informed by his boss that his monthly wages had been increased by the amount he had given to missions, and so he was able both to make his sacrificial gift to missions and to procure his needed suit of clothes.

Frank E. Burkhalter, *Living Abundantly* (Nashville: Convention Press, 1942), pp. 117-118.

## GIVING A PERSON BY GIVING MONEY

Dr. E. Y. Mullins once said: "The poor Scotch woman who, by hard labor and sacrifice, saved $60 and gave it to David Livingstone, the missionary and explorer, to provide for him an African body servant, was potentially a Livingstone. And when the body servant thus obtained saved Livingstone's life from the attack of a lion, she had given Livingstone for the remainder of his days."

Frank E. Burkhalter, *Living Abundantly* (Nashville: Convention Press, 1942), p. 123.

## MULTIPLYING ONE'S MINISTRY

Many years ago a brilliant young Englishman had dedicated himself to God and prepared himself for missionary service on the foreign fields. But when time came for his physical examination, the mission board's physician found that the young man's constitution could not stand the strain of the climate in equatorial Africa, where the candidate had hoped to invest his life. The mission board sustained the findings of the physician and refused to appoint the applicant to service.

The young man's disappointment almost broke his heart at first, but he had long ago learned to lay all his problems before the Lord. When he took this biggest matter of his life to the throne of grace, the Heavenly Father revealed to him that he had it within his power to become a great physician in London, and that by giving his income to the mission board he could make possible the sending of numerous missionaries to Africa instead of going out himself. The young man accepted the Lord's home assignment and succeeded in his medical profession in a marvelous manner; and many years ago this London physician had sent out sixty missionaries from his liberal professional income and thus multiplied his mission ministry sixtyfold by remaining at home.

Frank E. Burkhalter, *Living Abundantly* (Nashville: Convention Press, 1942), p. 122.

## SHARING IN THE WORK OF OTHERS

A Baptist merchant in North Carolina paid the salary of a Baptist missionary in China for many years. The missionary reported regularly concerning every phase of his work to this good layman who was supporting him. When the merchant wanted to acquaint others with the progress of this particular mission station in China he would always refer to the work there as "our" work. When he referred to the missionary he would characterize him as "my" missionary. Nor did this good layman exaggerate the situation. The work in China was actually his, in part, because his gifts made it possible, and this missionary was a partner of this merchant, who could not himself go and take the gospel message, just as he was also an ambassador of Jesus Christ. And when time ends and all the records of our work on earth are balanced in the books of heaven, this loyal merchant will find that he had had a share in the salvation of every soul whom the missionary won to Christ on the foreign field, and in every other good influence this man of God set in motion in the service of the Master.

Frank E. Burkhalter, *Living Abundantly* (Nashville: Convention Press, 1942), pp. 121-122.

## USING MATERIAL BLESSINGS TO BLESS OTHERS

The late J. F. Jarman, active Christian layman of Nashville, Tennessee, was for a number of years vice-president and sales manager of a large shoe factory in that city. He was a faithful steward and longed to see the day when he might own a factory himself and operate the business as he believed God would have him do. On several occasions, as the passing years would draw to a close, Mr. Jarman would approach the president of the concern and ask the privilege of resigning; but so valuable were his services to the business that the president would persuade him to stay with the concern by increasing both his salary and his commission.

Finally, as Mr. Jarman approached the age of sixty, he decided that if he was ever to establish himself a business of his own and operate it on a definitely Christian basis, he would have to do so soon; so he resolved to settle the matter once and for all.

Taking a day off from work in the interim between Christmas and New Year, this Christian businessman drove out to a little town not far from Nashville, engaged a room at a hotel, and instructed the clerk that he must not be disturbed by anyone or any type of call or interruption at any hour that day.

Entering the room, Mr. Jarman got down on his knees before his open Bible, read a number of passages from the book, and then prayed earnestly that God would reveal to him unmistakably what his will for him was in the matter of going into business for himself. As the day wore on, this good man received what he interpreted as a definite answer from God that he should relinquish all connections with the older firm, enter business for himself, and take God into his partnership in the conduct of his factory and in the disposition of the profits of the concern.

Having received his answer from the Lord, Mr. Jarman lost no time in acting upon it by resigning promptly all previous connections with the older shoe company and launching a business of his own. After securing a site and building his factory in Nashville, he got his business under way about the middle of August and made a net profit in excess of $20,000 by the end of the year. Businessmen recognize this record as a very unusual one.

The young business was fairly well established by the time the financial debacle of 1929 occurred, and throughout the depression that followed the sales of this company continued to mount until now the company is recognized as one of the major shoe companies of America.

Mr. Jarman had been a faithful tither for many years prior to going into business for himself. He believed his employees were entitled to adequate wages, the very best of working conditions, expert medical and dental service, and an opportunity to become shareholders in the company; so he promptly put these various provisions into operation.

Before he died in 1938 he had set up a foundation for the promotion of special Christian enterprises in which he was vitally interested, and so liberally had God prospered him in business he had been able to place more than a million dollars into that foundation, in addition to making adequate provision for the members of his family.

Frank E. Burkhalter, *Living Abundantly* (Nashville: Convention Press, 1942), pp. 118-119.

## SERVING THROUGH OTHERS

There was an old shoemaker who once had wished to become a minister, but the way had never opened up. He was the friend of a young divinity student; and when the lad one day was called to his first charge the old man asked him for one favor. He asked to be allowed always to make the lad's shoes, as long as life remained to him, so that he might feel that the preacher was wearing his shoes in the pulpit into which he could never come himself.

From *The Gospel of Luke,* translated and interpreted by William Barclay. Published in the U.S.A. by The Westminster Press, 1957, p. 96. Used by permission.

## THE VALUE OF ONE UNSELFISH ACT

Dostoievski wrote a classic story about a woman who died and was told that she would be taken to heaven if she could remember one unselfish act that she had performed while on earth. She could remember only one—a withered carrot that she had given to a beggar. So down the limitless space that separates heaven from hell the carrot was lowered on a slender string. Desperately she grasped it and slowly began to rise. Suddenly she felt a weight holding her back and, looking down, she saw other tormented souls clinging to her and hoping to rise with her. "Let go!" she cried. "This is *my carrot.*" At that point the string broke, and still clutching her precious carrot, the woman fell down into the pains of hell.

Leonard Griffith in *Encounters with Christ* (New York: Harper and Row, 1965), p. 122. Used by permission.

## WISE USE OF MONEY SHOWS WHERE HEAVEN IS

Dr. W. F. Powell, of Nashville, related this incident. He was going down to his office one Monday after making a call on a family that was in sore distress, when a well-to-do merchant called across the street to him. "Dr. Powell," he said, "you preached a great sermon on heaven yesterday. But you didn't tell us where heaven is."

Dr. Powell said, "I looked at him and his fine clothes and his beautiful store filled with all the good things to eat that anyone would want, and I thought of that family in need. I answered him rather sharply, 'Come over here and walk a couple of blocks with me, and I will show you where heaven is not but where it could be.' "

Dr. Powell pointed to a little yellow house on the side of a hill and said to him, "In that house are two children sick in bed and a mother, who is so sick she should be in bed. There isn't one thing to eat in that house. There isn't a piece of wood or a lump of coal. Walk up there and take a good look at their needs. Fill their pantry full of food; send them a load of coal and a load of wood. Get someone to go up there to take care of them and cook for them for a few days, and you will find out where heaven could be."

The next day he came into Dr. Powell's study, sat down, and looked at him silently for a couple of minutes. Then he said in a husky voice, "I'm mad at you. Why haven't you told me before where there was trouble like that? I did everything you suggested and then some, and I will look after them until their trouble is over. I just came from there. They are all smiles. They couldn't thank me enough. Now you don't have to tell me where heaven is; a little of it is in my heart."

C. Roy Angell, *God's Gold Mines* (Nashville: Broadman Press, 1962), pp. 13-14. Used by permission.

## AN ASSESSMENT OF VALUES

A hill shepherd's wife wrote a most interesting letter to a newspaper some time ago. Her children had been brought up in the loneliness of the hills. They were simple and unsophisticated. Then her husband got a position in a town and the children who had been brought up in the hills were introduced to the town. They changed and they changed very considerably— and they changed for the worse. The last paragraph of her letter reads like this—"Which is preferable for a child's upbringing—a lack of worldliness, but with better manners and sincere and simple thoughts, or worldliness and its present-day habit of knowing the price of everything and the value of nothing?"

From *The Gospel of Mark,* translated and interpreted by William Barclay. Published in the U.S.A. by The Westminster Press, 1957. p. 256. Used by permission.

# ... CONCERNING SOME EXAMPLES
# OF GIVING

### ETERNAL REVENUE

I work for the Department of Internal Revenue. Yes, I am the chap that everybody loathes. I go over income tax returns.

The other day I checked an unusual return. Some guy with an income under $5,000 claimed that he gave $624 to some church. Sure he was within the 15 percent limit—but it looked mighty suspicious to me. So I grabbed a bus and dropped in on the guy. Asked him about his "contributions."

I thought he'd get nervous like most of them do, and say that he "might have made a mistake." But not this guy! He came back at me with the figure of $624 without batting an eyelash. "Do you have a receipt from the church?" I asked, figuring that would make him squirm.

"Sure," he said. "I always drop them in the drawer where I keep my envelopes." So off he went to fetch his receipts.

Well, he had me! One look at the receipts and I knew he was on the level. So I apologized for bothering him, explaining that I have to check up on the deductions that seem unusually high. And as we shook hands at the door he said, "I'd like to invite you to attend our church sometime."

"Thanks," I replied, "but I belong to a church myself."

"Excuse me," he said, "that possibility had not occurred to me."

As I rode the bus home I kept wondering what he meant by that last remark. It was not until Sunday morning when I dropped my usual quarter into the collection plate, that it came to me.

B. W. Woods in the bulletin of the First Baptist Church, Seminole, Oklahoma.

## PROSPERITY OF LIFE

In the early days of my ministry, while I was a country preacher in North Carolina, I met one of God's own saints, Josiah Elliott. He, too, was a country preacher for over fifty years, and he raised the level of spiritual living over a great section of the state he loved. In the last two or three years of his life, when he couldn't preach or even leave his home, he lived on the fat of the land. Although he had never saved a cent of money, he had invested in sending young ministerial students through college. He even mortgaged his home five times, and the five boys for whom it was done paid back every cent of the money. They were the pallbearers at his funeral.

The people of the community built that proverbial road to his front door, and they kept his smokehouse and his pantry filled with all the good things to eat. It was not unusual to hear a pastor say on a Sunday morning in one of those country churches which Josiah Elliott had served, "Let's take a love offering today for Brother Josiah." Propped up in bed, the grand old man with his long gray-white beard looked like a prophet. People came, not only to bring him something nice, but they came to kneel by his bed and ask him to pray for them. I can still feel his hand on my head as I knelt with my face in the crazy quilt and heard him earnestly ask God to make me a good preacher and keep me humble. Josiah Elliott prospered in health; he prospered materially, for he wanted for nothing; he prospered spiritually; and the crowds that came smiling with gifts assured him of their affection and love. They did unto him *even as* he had done unto them. They brought him happiness and peace of mind.

C. Roy Angell, *The Price Tags of Life* (Nashville: Broadman Press, 1959), pp. 35-36. Used by permission.

## BETTER TO GIVE THAN TO RECEIVE: WHAT KIND OF BROTHER ARE YOU?

A businessman of San Antonio, one of the grandest Christians I ever knew, came over to my home late one night about two weeks after Christmas. As I opened the door I asked him, "What brings you out this time of evening?"

Smilingly he answered, "I've got to tell you something that made this Christmas the most wonderful one of my life." He got comfortable before the fire and began. "About four weeks ago my brother gave me a Packard automobile for a Christmas present. One evening a few days before Christmas, I came down out of my office and walked over to my car. There was a little street urchin walking around it touching it with a finger and looking in the windows. When I put the key in the door, he came around on my side. He was ragged and dirty and barefooted.

"He squinted up at me and said, 'Is this your automobile, mister?'

"I smiled at him and said, 'It sure is, son. Isn't it a beauty?'

" 'Mister, what did it cost?'

"When I told him I didn't know, he looked me up and down carefully and then spoke. 'Mister, you don't look like a man that would steal an automobile. Where did you get it?'

"With a bit of pride I told him, 'My brother gave it to me for a Christmas present.'

" 'You mean—' he said, 'you mean your brother gie it to you, and it didn't cost you nothing?'

"I said, 'That's right. My brother gie it to me, and it didn't cost me nothing.'

"He dug his toes down against the sidewalk for a minute and was lost in thought, then he began, 'I wist'—I knew what he was going to wish. He was going to wish he had a brother like that, and I had the answer ready for him. But he didn't say that, and what he did say jarred me all the way down to my heels. 'I wist I could be a brother like that.'

" 'What did you say?' I asked in astonishment.

"He repeated, 'I wist I could be a brother like that.'

"It confused me so that I couldn't find an answer, and I blurted out, 'Don't you want to ride in my automobile?'

"He looked at his clothes and answered, 'It's so pretty and clean, and I'm so dirty I would muss it up.'

*145*

" 'You might be dirty on the outside, but you're mighty clean on the inside. You will do my automobile good. Get in.'

"He wanted to know what everything on the panel board was, and I sat there and explained it to him. We hadn't gone far when he turned and with his eyes aglow said, 'Mister, would you mind driving in front of my house?' I smiled a little as I squeezed the big car down a half-alley and a half-street. I thought I knew what he wanted. I thought he wanted to show his neighbors that he could ride home in a big automobile, but I had him wrong again.

"He pointed ahead and said, 'Stop right where those two steps are. Will you stay here,' he asked, 'till I come back? It will be just a minute.' He ran up the steps, and then in a little while I heard him coming back, but he was not coming fast. He was coming down like he was carrying a load and putting his best foot down first and then the other one even with it. On the steps that came down on the inside I saw his feet first, and then I saw two more feet, withered and dangling. He was carrying his little brother. Infantile paralysis was written all over him. The well boy set his brother down on the bottom step and then sat down by him, sort of squeezed him up against him and pointed to the car.

" 'There she is, Buddy, just like I told you upstairs. His brother gie it to him, and it didn't cost him a cent, and some day I'm gonna gie you one.'

"I slowly climbed out and sat down by them. 'So that's the reason,' I said, 'that you wanted to be a brother like that?'

" 'Yes,' he answered. 'You see, the store windows are full of pretty things, and I try to remember them, but I can't tell him about them very well, and some day I'm gonna gie him a car so he can see them himself.'

"I said to them both, 'We won't wait until then. I'm going to put you both in the car and let you see them today, and I am going to let you pick out anything you want, and I'll buy it for you.' I put a Christmas tree up in that house and played Santa Claus for them. It was the grandest Christmas I ever had." He had learned what Jesus meant when he said, "It is more blessed to give than to receive."

C. Roy Angell, *Baskets of Silver* (Nashville: Broadman Press, 1955), pp. 95-98. Used by permission.

## FAITHFULNESS IN GIVING INSPIRES OTHERS

A young soldier by the name of Page was down in the sands of Egypt during World War II. When payday came he took his tithe and put it in an envelope and sent it to his mother with a note which said, "Give it to the preacher for the new Sunday School building so when I get home I can have a Sunday school room and not have to be in a class that sits in the auditorium. All of the boys in our class have wished for a room of our own, like a few of the adults have." Two years later the war was over and the boy started home. He called his mother and told her what train he would be on. There were nearly a thousand people at the station to meet him. He didn't think the crowd was for him, so he began looking to see who was behind him that all of these people had come to meet. Then his mother was in front of him, along with the preacher, a crowd of the deacons, and others. After they had greeted him, they said, "Now, before you go home, we're going to take you by the church. There is something we want you to see." They stopped his car in front of a beautiful educational building. Lo, and behold, carved in marble above the door was THE PAGE BUILDING. He stood there astonished and confused, and wept. Finally he asked, "Why did they name it after me?" The preacher answered, "I read that letter you wrote to your mother to the congregation one Sunday morning, and I held up the dollar bills you sent in your letter. The church took it from there. That letter, those dollar bills, and your faithful stewardship built that building. Your name *belongs* on it."

C. Roy Angell, *Rejoicing on Great Days* (Nashville: Broadman Press, 1963), pp. 15-16. Used by permission.

## "GIVE, AND IT SHALL BE GIVEN UNTO YOU"

I like to think of that lady who owned a toy shop in a

little city. Christmas was coming. Her capital was so small she had borrowed money to stock her counters with Christmas toys. Then there came a whisper of a depression and people stopped buying. She could see bankruptcy and failure facing her, for there were no customers. One little boy came every day and stopped at the same counter and longingly watched a toy merry-go-round as it merrily rotated. One day she walked over to him and said, "Sonny, is that what you want Santa Claus to bring you?" He answered, "Yes'm, that's what I want, but my father got hurt in an accident and Mother said there won't be much Christmas for us this year. So, I thought I'd come in each day, if you don't mind, and look at it until it's sold." And she said, "Bless your heart, play with it, if you want to. I have a lot more of them, so don't be uneasy. If that one is sold, I'll just put another one up there and keep it running."

He came in another day and another day and another day until one day she said to herself, He wants it so bad his eyes just sparkle; I'm going to give it to him. She walked over and picked it up and held it over the counter to him and said, "It's yours, from me to you. It's a Christmas present." His eyes got big and the tears of joy came running down his cheeks. He took it and hugged it up against him and took a few steps away and looked back to make sure she wasn't going to grab it out of his hand. Then he ran a few steps to the door and looked back again. He got outside the door and sat right down on the sidewalk, wound it up, and watched it spin.

A crowd gathered around and watched him enjoying it to its fullest. Then the crowd came inside. They bought every merry-go-round she had, and while they were there they bought other toys. When the counters were nearly empty, she said reverently, "I believe in God. I know there is a God, I believe in a God of justice, a good God, a God who will do what he says: 'Give, and it shall be given unto you; good measure, pressed down, and shaken together, and running over.' "

C. Roy Angell, *Rejoicing on Great Days* (Nashville: Broadman Press, 1968), pp. 23-24. Used by permission.

## WHEN HEARTSTRINGS ARE TOUCHED

When the heartstrings are touched people respond.

Last Sunday when we completed (and exceeded the goal) the Lottie Moon Christmas Offering for Foreign Missions we had several illustrations of what can happen when the heartstrings are touched.

After the 11:00 A.M. service Don Evans, our assistant pastor, was greeting people at one of the doors. A junior high school boy stopped and handing him a nickel said, "That's all the money I have. I want it to go to the Lottie Moon Offering." If I remember correctly, the widow gave all the money she had when she gave her mite.

Another boy had his ninth birthday last Sunday. An uncle and aunt had given him a check for two dollars for his birthday. When the money was counted Monday the money counting committee found one Lottie Moon Offering envelope with a personal check for two dollars in it. Across the back in the finest kind of third grade cursive writing was this boy's endorsement.

During the week I received a note from a college student with a twenty-dollar bill in it. The note indicated that the money was to go to the Lottie Moon Offering. It also said, "Please forgive me for waiting so long. It was practically a necessity that I wait until I received my scholarship money."

Yes, when the need is known and the heartstrings are touched people will do the noble thing. There is no way to estimate the good that can be done for the cause of Christ because of this extra effort from our people.

There is only one problem: Why are our heartstrings touched so seldom?

Think of all the people we could help; think of all the encouragement we could give; think of all the suffering we could relieve; think of all the witness to Christ we could give; think of all the projects we could complete *if* our heartstrings were touched. Keep your heart in tune with God so that the Holy Spirit can touch your heartstrings as needed.

JEC

## SACRIFICIAL GIVING SERVES AS AN
## EXAMPLE TO INSPIRE OTHERS TO GIVE

But experience, as well as the Scriptures, testifies to the fact that God never allows generous support of his causes to go unrewarded spiritually. During the conduct of the Baptist 75 Million Campaign in the fall of 1919, a very poor widow, operating a very small, rocky, unproductive hillside farm eleven miles from Asheville, North Carolina, heard of this forward movement in her denomination and prayed earnestly that the Lord would make it possible for her to have some share in that effort for the extension of his kingdom.

This dear, good woman, who was helping support a widowed daughter and three grandchildren, had only thirty cents in cash to her name; and the daughter had urged that this sum be used for buying some small Christmas tokens for the children in the home. But as the grandmother prayed she became convinced that it was her duty to give this thirty cents—all the money she had—to the campaign.

On the morning on which this aged widow had planned to drive into Asheville to give her offering to the treasurer of her church, she found that the sole work horse on the farm had a shoulder so sore he could not wear a collar. Not to be deterred from her purpose, the widow decided to walk the entire distance of twenty-two miles into town and back, and that in the rain, that she might be represented in her church's offering to the new program. And she actually trudged the whole distance without so much as a raincoat to protect her, as an old faded shawl was the only thing in the way of a wrap she possessed.

When she reached the treasurer's office and explained her circumstances and her desire, he at first refused to accept the thirty cents, assuring her the Lord would not have her practice such self-denial. But the widow assured him she had made the matter a subject of prayer for many days and that God had told her to give all she had. The treasurer was so rebuked by the widow's generosity that he told the dear woman he would quadruple his pledge; and on that Wednesday night when the offcer told the story to the church, many other members greatly incerased the amounts they had planned to give.

Soon the news of this sacrificial gift reached the denomination at large and, through the news agencies, the world at large; and several millions of additional money were pledged to the forward movement as a result of this country woman's liberality.

A newspaper syndicate heard of the story and sent one of its best correspondents to North Carolina to find the woman and interview her for a feature article that was sent all over America. The correspondent took a picture of the woman's humble home and family, told her circumstances in detail, and suggested that those feeling disposed to do so might send the woman and members of her family something for Christmas.

In an effort to check up on the responsiveness of the American public, the syndicate sent the same correspondent back to see the widow after Christmas and see what kind of holiday she and her family had enjoyed. The newspaper man found that general Christmas remembrances had come from all over America and that the dear widow, who had given her all to God, declared the presents had come from God. And had they not done so? Are we not persuaded that when this good saint stands before the judgment seat of Christ in the last day she will find a far larger blessing is hers than she could ever have anticipated? She will have a share in all the good that has been accomplished through the years by the additional millions of dollars given to God's cause from the inspiration produced by her giving all she had for the Master.

Frank E. Burkhalter, *Living Abundantly* (Nashville: Convention Press, 1942), pp. 30-32.

## A MODERN VERSION OF THE MACEDONIAN CHURCH SENDING AID TO JERUSALEM

In the little Methodist Chapel in the English village of Watlington there is an unusual collection of hymn books. Outwardly they resemble any other Methodist hymn books, but on the inside cover each bears this unique inscription: "Presented to the Watlington Methodist Church by the Chinese Methodist Churches of Hong Kong, 1953." Here is the story.

In 1952 there came to Watlington the Rev. Arthur Bray,

who for twenty-five years had been a distinguished missionary in China and who had returned to England to spend his few years before retirement in whatever small rural community needed him. He found a dismal situation in Watlington, a church building dreadfully dilapidated, the plaster crumbling off the walls, and the roof badly in need of repair. He tried to get the people to do something about it, but with no result; there were too few of them and they just didn't have the money. Even the Methodist Conference could promise no help.

One day, after a season of prayer, Arthur Bray wrote to some sympathetic friends in Hong Kong, sharing his problem with them and asking if they would care to assist privately. Before leaving the East he had helped them to build a church and he knew, as the Chinese knew, that the morale of Christian people rises when they have a house of worship of which they can be proud. These good friends not only sympathized. Like the Macedonians in Paul's letter, they welcomed the privilege of demonstrating their gratitude to the parent church which had given them birth and done so much for them. They canvassed the entire Chinese Methodist community in Hong Kong and collected sufficient funds to finance the repair and redecoration of the Watlington chapel as well as the provision of those hymn books containing their memorable inscription.

A. Leonard Griffith, *God and His People* (New York and Nashville: Abingdon Press, 1960), p. 63. Reprinted by permission of the publisher.

# ... CONCERNING THE DANGERS
# OF SELFISHNESS

## WILL LOSE EARTHLY TREASURE

Every penny, every ounce of treasure, that we invest in this world we are absolutely sure to lose.

This is true regardless of the nature of our treasure. If it is in money, we shall lose that. When, I do not know. It may be to-day, it may be to-morrow, but certainly we shall lose it some time. How we shall lose, I cannot say. The possibilities for such disaster are numerous. If we lose by no other process, then Highwayman Death will at last wrench it from our fingers and fling us empty-handed and poverty-stricken out into the night. Very often the loss comes before death. A few years ago a man was carrying water in a certain city for ten cents per hour. Yet, that man owned a mausoleum that cost him two hundred thousand dollars. He had builded it in the days of his prosperity, but reverses had come. Now he had nothing left but a resting place for his dead body.

Clovis G. Chappell, *The Sermon on the Mount* (New York and Nashville: Abingdon Press, 1930), p. 185. Reprinted by permission of the publisher.

## WHEN ALL YOUR TREASURE IS MATERIAL

Years ago there lived near my old home a man who was a thorough-going miser. He worked hard and spent little and gave nothing. In this manner he managed to accumulate some five thousand dollars in gold. He would not deposit this money in a bank. He hid it in a secret place known only to himself. But one night a highwayman paid him a visit. He stuck the muzzle of an angry-looking gun close up against the man's face and asked him for a donation. The miser consented. He gave him every dollar, though it broke his heart. "Why did you not argue the question with him?" an old friend asked the next day. "Why did you not refuse?" "Hell was too close," was the simple answer. All this man's treasure was on the outside of him. None was in his heart.

Clovis G. Chappell, *The Sermon on the Mount* (New York and Nashville: Abingdon Press, 1930), p. 188. Reprinted by permission of the publisher.

## HAD HE THE GOLD, OR HAD THE GOLD HIM?

Francis G. Peabody in one of his Harvard addresses told Ruskin's story of a man who tried to swim to safety from a wrecked ship. About his waist he tied a belt containing two hundred pounds in gold, money which he could not bring himself to leave behind. Unable to reach shore with the extra weight, he sank and was drowned. Ruskin asked, "As he was sinking, had he the gold, or had the gold him?"

*Interpreter's Bible* (Nashville: Abingdon Press, 1955), XI, p. 452. Reprinted by permission of the publisher.

## GAINING POSSESSIONS AT THE EXPENSE OF STILL HIGHER DUTIES

Robertson Nicoll, the great editor, was born in a manse in the north-east of Scotland. His father had one great passion, to buy and to read books. He was a minister and he never had more than 200 pounds a year. But he amassed the greatest private library in Scotland amounting to 17,000 books. He did not use them in his sermons; he was simply consumed to own and read them. When he was forty he married a girl of twenty-four. In eight years she was dead of tuberculosis; of a family of five only two lived to be over twenty. That cancerous growth of books filled every room and every passage in the manse. It may have delighted the owner of the books, but it killed his wife and family. There are possessions which can be acquired at too great a cost.

From *The Gospel of Matthew,* Vols. 1 & 2, translated and interpreted by William Barclay. Published in the U.S.A. by The Westminster Press, 1959. I, p. 256. Used by permission.

## GAINING POSSESSIONS AT THE RISK
## OF HONOR AND HONESTY

George Macdonald tells of a village shop-keeper who grew very rich. Whenever he was measuring cloth, he measured it with his two thumbs inside the measure so that he always gave short measure. George Macdonald says of him, "He took from his soul, and he put it in his siller-bag." A man can enrich his bank account at the expense of impoverishing his soul.

From *The Gospel of Matthew,* Vols. 1 & 2, translated and interpreted by William Barclay. Published in the U.S.A. by The Westminster Press, 1959. I, p. 256. Used by permission.


## THE CORRUPTING INFLUENCE OF TOO
## MUCH FINANCIAL SECURITY

James Barrie wrote a little half-hour play entitled "The Will." A young couple enter a lawyer's office to draw up a will. They are bride and groom, and very happy. The husband, Philip Ross, has inherited some money and wants to make the will in a single sentence, leaving everything to his wife. She lovingly protests at being made the sole beneficiary, and insists on a clause by which their little wealth would be shared with his cousins and a convalescent home. The lawyer, deeply impressed with their refreshing unselfishness, pats them on the back as they leave: "You are a ridiculous couple. But don't change."

Twenty years later they come back to make a new will, now involving a sizable estate. The wife has come along to see that the husband does nothing foolish; she wrangles with him when he wants to include his cousins, and the poor convalescent home is dropped completely. Each refers to the estate as "my money," and only after bitter argument is any agreement reached at all.

Twenty years more, and *Sir* Philip Ross, knighted now, and sixty-five years old, comes in alone. She is dead. The children, he says, have turned out to be "rotters." This time he has come to cancel all previous wills, cutting off all his relatives without a penny. He starts to dictate to the lawyer, "I leave it

—leave it—my God, I don't know what to do with it!" He paces the floor and at last shouts angrily, "Here are the names of half a dozen men I fought to get my money. I beat them. Leave it to *them,* with my curses."

J. Wallace Hamilton, *Ride the Wild Horses!* (Westwood, N.J.: Fleming H. Revell Company, 1952), pp. 57-58. Reprinted by permission of the publisher.

## THE PASSION TO POSSESS SOON POSSESSES THE MAN

Tolstoy describes the pathos of this in his story of the man with the land-hunger. The man started out at the first blush of dawn, with the promise that he could have for his own all the land he could walk around from sunrise to sunset. He began leisurely enough, glad for his sturdy legs; then the lure of the black soil stirred the thought in him that by quickening his pace he could encircle more land. The farther he went, the faster he went. He burned with fever; one word, "More!" echoed in his brain and heart. At last the sun was low in the west, and his legs began to fail him. He threw off his blouse and his boots and he felt his heart beating like a drum, but forcing his body to the utmost, just as the sun fell beyond the horizon, he flung himself forward with his fingertips touching the goal, and dropped there—dead. They took a shovel and gave him his land, a strip of soil six by two. It is a faithful parable of that fierce drive for "more!" for which men barter and lose their immortal souls.

J. Wallace Hamilton, *Ride the Wild Horses!* (Westwood, N.J.: Fleming H. Revell Company, 1952), pp. 54-55. Reprinted by permission of the publisher.

## MONEY MICROBE

Two scientists made a series of bacteriological experiments on paper money after it had been in circulation a short time. Nineteen hundred germs of various kinds were found on the average bank note, and one microbe was discovered which was peculiar to paper money in that it had never been found anywhere else. It seemed to thrive and multiply only on the kind of paper out of which money is made. So it might be said, by way of a parable, that there is a money microbe.

Walter Dudley Cavert, *Remember Now . . .* (New York: Abingdon Press, 1944), p. 142, cited in *The Life and Work Lesson Annual,* 1969-70 (Nashville: Convention Press, 1969), pp. 218-219. Used by permission.

## ECONOMIC ATHEISM

Let us take a moment to look at another form of atheism in the area of stewardship, in our relationship to the material world. We can call it economic atheism. Certainly the question here is one of sovereignty. Who is God? Who owns the earth? Who is first for us with reference to our money and material possessions? To whom does the world with its vast store of resources really belong? That is a basic question, and there is no concealing our atheism here. Seek ye first the Kingdom of God? Our national income stands at over three hundred billion; our contributions to all God's causes approximates two per cent. First? A little girl, watching her father total up his income tax, noticed the difference between the tax to the government and his gifts to the church, and said, "Look, Daddy, Uncle Sam gets more than God." Liquor gets more than God in America; luxury, movies, tobacco, even cosmetics get more than Christ and Christ's church. First? We spend more on the skins of women than on the souls of mankind. We are not monotheists yet. We believe in God, but give our money to the other gods.

And yet we know that all this is just a symptom of the sickness. The real sickness is deeper. The great blasphemy of man, the real sin and atheism of his streaky heart, is his denial in practice that the world belongs to God and that it is to be used for God's purposes; his assumption that the world is his, to serve his ends and do with as he pleases. That is the great lie in the mind of man, and out of it come all his other illusions. That is the false idea that won't let anything else come right.

J. Wallace Hamilton, *Who Goes There?* (Westwood, N.J.: Fleming H. Revell Company, 1958), pp. 44-45. Reprinted by permission of the publisher.

## MONEY DOES NOT BRING HAPPINESS

Somebody asked Cecil Rhodes, who certainly in the nineteenth century was one of the richest men in Northern Rhodesia, if he were happy. "No, I'm not happy," he said. "I've spent half of my life and half of my money giving it to the doctor keeping me out of the grave and the other half to the lawyer to keep me out of jail."

Gaston Foote, Fort Worth, Texas, in a chapel address at Southwestern Baptist Theological Seminary, November 16, 1960. Used by permission.


## RESULT OF A LIFE BUILT ON THE MATERIAL

There is a legend of a wealthy man who was one day visited by an angel. The angel told the man that he could have any request granted that he wished. The broker asked for a newspaper dated one year from that day. The request was immediately granted. The man thumbed through the paper to the financial page and said, "Look, I made $10,000 yesterday. Isn't that wonderful?" The angel turned the paper back several pages and said, "But look, here is the acount of your funeral. You died three days ago."

Fred M. Wood, *Bible Truth in Person* (Nashville: Broadman Press, 1965), p. 85. Reprinted by permission of the author.


## MONEY IS TEMPORARY, NOT ETERNAL

Cornelius Vanderbilt was a great tycoon in American life. He knew how to make money but he never knew how to invest it. As an octogenarian he retired at Asheville, North Carolina. He lived at the Biltmore Estates. He loved roses, and early one morning he was out in the rose garden and a cry, seemingly of distress, came from his throat. And a nurse went out there and said, "What's the matter, Mr. Vanderbilt, are you ill?" He said, "No, no, I'm not ill and I'm sorry I disturbed you. I was looking at these hands, these hands which have written checks for a million, two million, or five million dollars, and now there's just nothing in them, just nothing."

Everything that passed through his hands just passed through. He never learned to invest in the things which are eternal. This business of Christian stewardship is taking those things which are temporary, such as money, and investing them in people or things which are eternal and never die. . . . But he never learned that.

Gaston Foote, Fort Worth, Texas, in a chapel address at Southwestern Baptist Theological Seminary, November 16, 1960. Used by permission.

# PART III
# SOME STEWARDSHIP SAYINGS

# ... ABOUT THE MEANING OF STEWARDSHIP

## MONEY IS NOT SYNONYMOUS WITH STEWARDSHIP

One who is a good steward dollar-wise is more often than not a good steward of all "the manifold grace of God" (I Peter 4:10). But not necessarily so! Money is not synonymous with stewardship, and the sooner we make material wealth a segment of stewardship rather than its synonym the sooner we approach the true meaning of accountability of all men before God.

Robert J. Hastings, *My Money and God* (Nashville: Broadman Press, 1961), pp. 11-12. Reprinted by permission of the author.

The most important aspect of tithing and stewardship is not the raising of money for church activity but the development of Christian character.

Fred M. Wood, *Bible Truth in Person* (Nashville: Broadman Press, 1965), p. 85. Reprinted by permission of the author.

## STEWARDSHIP ACKNOWLEDGES THE CLAIMS OF GOD

Stewardship, if true, must acknowledge that to be in the kingdom of God—to be under his sovereign rule—is to be under the absolute and ultimate claims of God.

Frank Stagg, *New Testament Theology* (Nashville: Broadman Press, 1962), p. 288. Used by permission.

## STEWARDSHIP: CONFIDENCE SPENDING

Perhaps we might call the awakened sense of Christian stewardship an example of "confidence spending." People give more generously to the Church because they want to express a vote of confidence in the Church. They have confidence that the Church is in actual truth the Body of Christ, not just another fraternity or service club. They have confidence that the whole Church is the Body of Christ and that not even the smallest member in the remotest corner of the earth can suffer without the whole body becoming weaker. They have confidence that the Church has a Gospel of salvation to a world on the dizzy edge of disaster and that there is no other name than the name of Jesus Christ by which the world may be saved from the final explosion.

A. Leonard Griffith, *God and His People* (New York and Nashville: Abingdon Press, 1960), p. 67. Reprinted by permission of the publisher.

God's first desire:

"What does Jesus want of us? He wants nothing of us but that we come. He does not want *ours* but *us.*"

Karl Barth, "Repentance," in *The Protestant Pulpit,* Andrew W. Blackwood, ed., (Nashville: Abingdon Press, 1957), p. 178. Reprinted by permission of the publisher.

The true disciple of Jesus is neither a miser nor a spend-thrift, but a steward.

William Hiram Foulkes.

## THE PROBLEM OF RELIGION

To be able to live a spiritual life in the midst of a material environment has been and is the perpetual problem of religion.

E. Stanley Jones, *The Christ of the Mount* (New York and Nashville: Abingdon Press, 1931), p. 220. Reprinted by permission of the publisher.

## SHARING IN GOD'S WORK

We are not invited to *support* God's enterprise but to share in it, to be partners with all who have served Christ through the centuries and all who serve Him in the world today.

A. Leonard Griffith, *This Is Living* (Nashville: Abingdon Press, 1966), p. 153. Reprinted by permission of the publisher.

As to all that we have and are, we are but stewards of the Most High God. —On all our possessions, on our time, and talents, and influence, and property, he has written, "Occupy for me, and till I shall come."—To obey his instructions and serve him faithfully, is the true test of obedience and discipleship.

Charles Simmons.

## STEWARDSHIP IS INCLUSIVE:
## IT INCLUDES EVERY ASPECT OF LIFE

Once we become thoroughly convinced that we belong to God, then it will be relatively easy for us to understand that our stewardship includes every aspect of our lives. We are not only stewards or trustees of the material things we possess; we are also stewards of life itself and all the experiences that come with life. This means, among other things, that we are responsible unto God for what we let sorrow and suffering, joy and happiness, do to and through our lives.

T. B. Maston, *Suffering: A Personal Perspective* (Nashville: Broadman Press, 1967), p. 60. Reprinted by permission of the author.

Christian Stewardship is the matching of gift for matchless gift: our life and its whole substance for the gift of perfect love. And though God's Son and His precious death are matchless—in the strange economy of God our gift returned is made sufficient. My all for His all. Stewardship is your commitment; the asking of God to take you back unto Himself—all that you have and all that you are.

Lawrence L. Furgin.

Stewardship is what a man does after he says, "I believe."

W. H. Greever.

It is not the weight of jewel or plate,
Or the fondle of silk or fur;

'Tis the spirit in which the gift is rich,
   As the gifts of the Wise Ones were,
And we are not told whose gift was gold,
   Or whose was the gift of myrrh.

Edmund Vance Cooke.


The world asks, How much does he give? Christ asks, Why does he give?

John Raleigh Mott.


Stewardship is the acceptance from God of personal responsibility for all of life and life's affairs.

Roswell C. Long.


God has never had on His side a majority of men and women. He does not need a majority to work wonders in history, but He does need a minority fully committed to Him and His purpose. In the world today Christian stewardship is a necessity.

Ernest Fremont Tittle.


God has given us two hands—one to receive with and the other to give with. We are not cisterns made for hoarding; we are channels made for sharing.

Billy Graham.


## GOD OWNS THE EARTH

Who owns the earth? The Communists say it belongs to the workers. The Socialists say it belongs to the State. The capitalists say it belongs to those who are smart enough and strong enough and free enough to take it. And because all are wrong in their basic outlook—that is, in their ideas of sovereignty—they will go on setting tribe against tribe in endless economic confusion. "The earth is the Lord's." That is not

166

good advice; it is the great truth, to which we must adjust, and without which nothing else will come right.

J. Wallace Hamilton, *Who Goes There?* (Westwood, New Jersey: Fleming H. Revell Company, 1958), pp. 45-46. Reprinted by permission of the publisher.

## GIVING AS FELLOWSHIP

"Contribution" renders the word *koinonian* [in Romans 15:26]. One of the great words for Christian relationships, it is often translated "Fellowship." Basically it meant a sharing or having all things in common, both privileges and responsibilities. As used here it speaks of sharing in material goods as an evidence of love, concern, and unity in Christ. They sought to share in and relieve the suffering of the "poor saints" in Jerusalem.

Herschel H. Hobbs, *Studying Life and Work Lessons,* January, February, March, 1969 (Nashville: Convention Press, 1968), p. 101. Used by permission.

Our children, relations, friends, honors, houses, lands, and endowments, the goods of nature and fortune, nay, even of grace itself, are only lent. It is our misfortune and our sin to fancy they are given. We start, therefore, and are angry when the loan is called in. We think ourselves masters, when we are only stewards, and forget that to each of us it will one day be said, "Give an account of thy stewardship."

Thomas H. Horne.

# . . . ABOUT THE TITHE

## JESUS' CONCERN ABOUT MEN AND THE MATERIAL

Jesus seemed to have two basic concerns with reference to a man and the material—that a man be free from the tyranny of things and that he be actively concerned for the needs of his brother.

Frank Stagg, *New Testament Theology* (Nashville: Broadman Press, 1962), p. 285. Used by permission.

## ROOTING TITHING IN THE GRACE OF GOD

As a voluntary system, tithing offers much; but it must be redeemed by grace if it is to be Christian. To plead that "it works" is only to adopt the pragmatic tests of the world. Much "works" that is not Christian. Tithing, if it is to be congenial to New Testament theology, must be rooted in the grace and love of God.

Frank Stagg, *New Testament Theology* (Nashville: Broadman Press, 1962), p. 293. Used by permission.

## AN EXPLANATION OF THE TITHE

Tithing is not, except derivatively, a plan for raising money. It is rather a ritual act through which man testifies to, and at the same time cultivates in himself, the spiritual dedication of which the overt giving of money or goods is but the adequate and impressive symbol.

Howard Foshee, "The Tithe," *Encyclopedia of Southern Baptists* (Nashville: Broadman Press, 1958), II, 1418. Used by permission.

## BIBLICAL TEACHINGS ABOUT THE TITHE

There is no question but that the Old Testament teaches

the tithe as the basis of religious giving. But even it teaches both "tithes and offerings" (Mal. 3:8).

However, the picture is not so clear in the New Testament. Some see the New Testament as not teaching the tithe. But one asks if the Christian should give less under grace than the Jew did under the law. The New Testament teaches that all of one's possessions belong to God. Did not the Old Testament do likewise?

Herschel H. Hobbs, *Studying Life and Work Lessons,* January, February, March, 1969 (Nashville: Convention Press, 1968), p. 98. Used by permission.

## JESUS AND TITHING

What about Jesus and the tithe? He commended the Pharisees for tithing but condemned their spirit in doing so (Matt. 23:23). He did not say in so many words that one should tithe. Neither did he forbid giving the tithe. Why should he tell Jews to do what they were doing already? In his death he fulfilled the Levitical law. But the tithe antedated that law (Gen. 14:20). It was basic in God's plan of stewardship. Wherever Jesus dealt with a law he went beyond the letter to the spirit (Matt. 5:17 ff.). Had he dealt with the law of tithing he probably would have done the same with it.

Did Jesus tithe? He was brought up in a godly Jewish home where most likely the tithe was given. He was familiar with the book of Deuteronomy which taught the tithe. He never broke one of God's laws. The tithe was one of the most sacred things to the Pharisees. They never criticized Jesus for not tithing. Had he neglected to do so, it is hard to believe that they would have overlooked that fact. A stronger case can be made that Jesus tithed than that he did not.

Herschel H. Hobbs, *Studying Life and Work Lessons,* January, February, March, 1969 (Nashville: Convention Press, 1968), pp. 98-99. Used by permission.

## PAUL'S TEACHING ABOUT TITHING

It is pointed out that in Paul's teaching on stewardship,

he did not command the tithe. Would one who had been a strict Pharisee blameless before the law have neglected this practice as a Jew? As for his teachings, it should be noted that in 1 Cornithians 16:1 ff. and 2 Corinthians 8 and 9 he was not dealing with basic church finances. He was taking an over-and-above offering for relief. Other than the argument from silence, the weakest of all arguments, there is a no real basis for claiming that either Jesus or Paul did not believe in and teach both "tithes and offerings." There is no lower standard of giving taught in the Bible.

Herschel H. Hobbs, *Studying Life and Work Lessons,* January, February, March, 1969 (Nashville: Convention Press, 1968), p. 98. Used by permission.

## WHY I TITHE

With my tithe I seal a bargain,
With my tithe I pay a debt.
With my tithe I serve a purpose
That my God will not forget.

With my tithe I fish for sinners,
With my tithe I find the lost.
With my tithe I gird the winners,
With my tithe I share the cost.

With my tithe I love my neighbor,
With my tithe I pass a test.
With my tithe I clothe His image
In a form one-tenth divine.

With my tithe I build a temple,
With my tithe I feed its fire.
With my tithe I still a yearning
Of my soul's innate desire.

With my tithe I heal the stricken,
With my tithe they rise again.
With my tithe I walk with giants,
In the wake of Godly men.

With my tithe I walk in honor
Where the great and strong
have trod
With my tithe I store my treasures
In the treasure house of God!

—Peter E. Long

Reprinted from "Lakeshore Leader," the bulletin of Lakeshore Baptist Church, Shreveport, Louisiana.

## SOME INTERESTING THOUGHTS ON TITHING

Tithing is an Old Testament word. It means tenth—a tenth of something: a tenth of the crop, a tenth of the money, a tenth of the grape harvest, a tenth of the land, or a tenth of the cattle, etc. The Old Testament Hebrews paid it with the regularity that we pay our income taxes, and with about as much spiritual meaning.

So when Jesus came on the scene he upgraded giving; instead of the tenth he demanded a new perspective on *all* of life. He commended the widow who gave *all* she had. He said nothing to the tithers. When the early Christians were being fed to the lions, Paul didn't talk about tithing either. That would be like showing Mickey Mantle how to hold the bat. But the New Testament didn't do away with the Old Testament standard; it simply upgraded it.

Now, frankly, I'm not up to the New Testament standard yet. I'm too tightly tied to that which is around me. Perhaps someday, if I keep working at it, I will be able to live consistently on a New Testament level.

But I have discovered that I can reach the Old Testament level, and that is something. I can give a tithe. As a materialist talking to other materialists, tithing isn't farfetched at all. It's a good step to conquering our greed and selfishness.

There is no convenient time to start tithing. You certainly will not begin when you have all your bills paid. Something will always be left out. I hope it is not the Lord.

James Flaming, Pastor, First Baptist Church, Abilene, Texas, in his church bulletin. Reprinted by permission of the author.

## "WHAT TITHING MEANS TO ME"

*This is what Coach Frank Broyles of the No. 1 Arkansas Razorbacks football team had to say in a recent article featured in* The Christian Athlete.

*All of life involves stewardship....* Tithing is the best way to acknowledge that God owns all I possess. I am His child; He has made it possible for me to live in this universe. I do not own it; He does. He sustains me daily. My tithe, given freely, gladly, and with love, is my acknowledgment that He is my Father and I belong to Him. I like to think of tithing as a matter of trust in the goodness and mercy of God in the days ahead. God has given us wealth abundantly—all we need and more. He trusts us to be good stewards. My regular giving of the tithe is an acknowledgment of my appreciation for His gifts and also of His faith in me to be a good steward in all He has intrusted to me. The tithe not only helps me acknowledledge God as Father, but also helps me use wisely the other nine-tenths.

I am happy to be a tither. My tithe helps my church carry forth the Lord's work and it helps me to handle carefully not only my money but all other gifts with which God has blessed me. I have never known a tither to be a miser. I have never known a tither to be an unhappy man. I have never known a tither who felt he was wasting his money. On the other hand, the tithers I have known have had a love for God. They have expressed a loyalty to the church and Kingdom and they have found joy in the handling of our God-given treasures.

I want to be a good steward. Tithing helps me in this and therefore I recommend it. Study it—pray about it—try it for a year. See for youself its real spiritual value to your life and the work of the Kingdom.

Frank Broyles
Head Football Coach
University of Arkansas

## WHEN TO START TITHING—NOW

If you are not now a tither, do not expect that a sudden

increase of income would make it easy for you to start. It won't—because you'll always find something to spend it for. Unless you tithe on your present income, it is highly doubtful if you would tithe on a higher one. There is only one way for most families to tithe: *set it aside.* We must be specific and exact, or we will be trivial and spasmodic. Benevolent dollars must be budgeted and protected the same as the food dollar, the health dollar, or any other.

Robert J. Hastings, *How To Manage Your Money* (Nashville: Broadman Press, 1965), p. 88. Reprinted by permission of the author.

## TITHING FAMILIES KNOW WHAT IS VITAL

In her book *Spending for Happiness,* Elsie Stapleton describes her contacts as a budget counselor with two hundred tithing families. All two hundred impressed her, for never did she find even one in the red. They allocated their money sensibly, and she was impressed with how well-adjusted they were financially as well as spiritually. "They knew the value of money, and they spent their earnings on what was most important to them. The 10 percent tithe was the most vital of their outlays." Looking at a lost, hungry world in the spirit of the Good Shepherd, can a Christian family give less than 10 percent?

Robert J. Hastings, *How To Manage Your Money* (Nashville: Broadman Press, 1965), p. 86. Reprinted by permission of the author.

## A PLEDGING PARODY

To pledge or not to pledge—that is the question.
Whether 'tis nobler in a man
To take the gospel free and let another foot the bill,
Or sign a pledge and pay toward church expenses!
To give, to pay—aye, there's the rub. To pay,
When on the free-pew plan, a man may have
A sitting free and take the gospel too,
As though he paid, and none be aught the wiser
Save the Finance Committee, who—
Most honourable of men—can keep a secret!

To err is human, and human, too, to buy
At cheapest rate. I'll take the gospel so!
For others do the same—a common rule!
I'm wise. I'll wait, not work—I'll pray, not pay,
And let the other fellow foot the bills,
And so I'll get the gospel free, you see!

A. Leonard Griffith, *God's Time and Ours* (London: Lutterworth Press, 1964), p. 195. Reprinted by permission of the publisher.

# ... ABOUT ATTITUDES TOWARD
MONEY AND GIVING

## STINGINESS TOWARD GOD

Martin Luther accused his congregation of downright stinginess. Because some of them begrudged even four pennies a week, he thundered from the pulpit, "You ungrateful beasts, you are not worthy of the treasures of the Gospel. If you don't improve, I will stop preaching rather than cast pearls before swine."

Cited in A. Leonard Griffith, *God and His People* (New York and Nashville: Abingdon Press, 1960), p. 67. Reprinted by permission of the publisher.

Rudyard Kipling told a group of graduates to be certain that they do not care too much for the material, because some day they would meet a man who cares not for it at all and then they would realize how poor they are.

Fred M. Wood, *Bible Truth in Person* (Nashville: Broadman Press, 1965), p. 85. Reprinted by permission of the author.

A fool may make money but it requires a wise man to spend it.

Ancient proverb.

## MONEY IS THE ACID TEST
FOR DETERMINING A CHRISTIAN'S SENSE OF VALUES

There are many tests which may be applied to determine a Christian's sense of values or that to which he is committed in his life. But, as someone has said, money is the acid test. This may be expanded to involve all material possessions or aspirations. Do these things take priority over spiritual values?

To what should one be committed if he is to live a rich Christian life?

Herschel H. Hobbs, *Studying Life and Work Lessons,* July, August, September, 1969 (Nashville: Convention Press, 1969), p. 56. Used by permission.

## HOW MONEY IS MADE

From the day they enter the church people are given an opportunity to give money, but they get so little guidance in how they make it.

Kenneth Chafin, *Help! I'm a Layman* (Waco: Word Books, 1966), p. 29. Used by permission of the publisher.

Money is like an arm or leg—use it or lose it.

Henry Ford.

## DIFFERENCE IN BEING RESPECTABLE AND IN BEING CHRISTIAN

It may be respectable never to take anything from anyone. It is Christian to give everything to someone.

From *The Gospel of Mark,* translated and interpreted by William Barclay. Published in the U.S.A. by The Westminster Press, 1957. p. 253. Used by permission.

## TWO IMPORTANT QUESTIONS ABOUT POSSESSIONS

There are two great questions about possessions, and on the answer to these questions everything depends.

(i) How did a man gain his possessions? Did he gain them in a way that he would be glad that Jesus Christ should see, or did he gain them in a way that he would wish to hide from Jesus Christ? ...

(ii) How does a man use his possessions? ... It is characteristic of God to give, and, if in our lives giving always ranks above getting, we will use aright what we possess, however much or however little it may be.

From *The Gospel of Matthew,* Vols. 1 & 2, translated and interpreted by William Barclay. Published in the U.S.A. by The Westminster Press, 1959. I, pp. 256-257. Used by permission.

## POSSESSIONS CAN BE A CHAIN OR A CROWN

If a man looks on his possessions as being given to him for nothing but his own comfort and convenience, then his possessions are a chain which must be broken: if a man looks at his possessions as a means to helping others, then his possessions are his crown.

From *The Gospel of Matthew,* Vols. 1 & 2, translated and interpreted by William Barclay. Published in the U.S.A. by The Westminster Press, 1959. II, p. 238. Used by permission.

## THE ISSUE: TO CELEBRATE GOD'S CREATION WITHOUT MAKING IT AN IDOL

The issue is not simply what we can get out of giving or even how much we will contribute to the church. The question rather is whether we can stand with unwithered values in the blast of a society that has an almost insatiable itch for things. *To celebrate God's creation without turning it into an idol*—that is a challenge which commands all of the urgency the pulpit can muster.

William E. Hull, *Baptist Standard,* Nov. 8, 1967. Used by permission of the publisher.

## THE TRAGEDY OF VALUING POSSESSIONS ABOVE PERSONALITY

In Dante's Hell not a single sinner in the Circle of the Avaricious can be identified. All of them are nameless, faceless. The man who values possessions above personality finds his Nemesis in the ultimate loss of his own personality. For a few acres of land and a few bags of gold he surrenders everything that could make him a person, a child of God through eternity.

Leonard Griffith, *Encounters with Christ* (New York: Harper and Row, 1965), p. 126. Used by permission.

Get to know two things about a man—how he earns his money and how he spends it—and you have the clue to his character, for you have a searchlight that shows up the inmost recesses of his soul. You know all you need to know about his standards, his motives, his driving desires, his real religion.

Robert James McCracken.

There are no pockets in a shroud.

Spanish proverb.

The use of money is all the advantage there is in having money.

Benjamin Franklin.

It's not what you'd do with a million,
If riches should e'er be your lot,
But what are you doing at present
With the dollar and a quarter you've got?

Anonymous.

He dropped a nickel in the plate,
Then meekly raised his eyes;
Glad that his weekly rent was paid
For a mansion in the skies.

Anonymous.

God loves a cheerful giver, but we settle for a grudging one.

Mildred McAfee Horton.

# A PARABLE

And he told them a story about a fellow.

This man had a pretty good year. His work went well and to himself and to most folks he was a success. (To people in some parts of the world he looked like a king.)

He was feeling real good, thinking about how hard he'd worked and how the results were finally showing. So he thumbed through the evening paper to the stock market report and looked over what he might invest in. And he could still hear his wife complaining about the house being too small to be comfortable, so he went through the real estate section too.

And he said to himself, "By George, there are lots bigger and better things we can pay down on now. Old buddy, you've scrimped and saved; it's time you started enjoying it! Just lean back in front of the TV and think about all the things you've got."

But just as he dozed off during a commercial, God called him by his first name, and his world crashed in around him. When God spoke to him, God called him a fool, and the man had to leave his reclining chair that very night, without time to pack a single suitcase or go by the bank. All he could take with him was himself—just what he was. Everything that was so important a few minutes ago suddenly didn't mean a thing.

So the story ended with the fellow who was feeling pretty well set left facing a different life. And he was realizing for the first time that by God's living standards he was flat broke.

Reprinted from the bulletin of the Western Hills Baptist Church, Fort Worth, Texas.

He gives nothing but worthless gold
Who gives from a sense of duty.

James Russell Lowell.

He who gives when he is asked has waited too long.

Anonymous.

It is not the shilling I give you that counts, but the warmth that it carries with it from my hand.

Miguel De Unamuno.

For too many giving is occasional, spasmodic, ill-proportioned. It depends on what is left over when other things have had their full share. Sometimes what it means is that only the small change lying in their pockets goes to the support of good and worthy causes.

Robert J. McCracken.

William Allan White, editor of Emporia, Kansas, once said, "There are three kicks in every dollar; one, when you make it; two, when you have it and third, when you give it away. The big kick is the last one." He had just given a 50-acre plot of ground along a river just outside the city to be used as a park. He offers quite a contrast to the lady who was considered by her neighbors to be in dire poverty, but after her death it was discovered that she was worth more than half a million dollars and yet lived a life of starvation. She shared with no one.

Ira H. Peak in "Lakeshore Leader," the bulletin of the Lakeshore Baptist Church, Shreveport, Louisiana.

## HOW MUCH WEALTH IT TAKES TO SATISFY

Someone asked Mr. Rockefeller, "How much wealth does it take to satisfy a man?" He answered, "Just a little more."

J. Wallace Hamilton, *Ride the Wild Horses!* (Westwood, N.J.: Fleming H. Revell Company, 1952), p. 54. Reprinted by permission of the publisher.

## EMPTINESS OF THE MATERIAL

He toiled and saved his earnings every day,
But starved his mind, and grasped at common things;
His prisoned soul ne'er struggled out of clay,
His better nature never found its wings.

He hoped to sit with Happiness at last,
Mansioned, sufficient, when he would be old;
But he was just a graveyard! and the past
Left naught for him but a rude pile of gold.

Louis Fraser

Fred M. Wood, *Bible Truth in Person* (Nashville: Broadman Press, 1965), pp. 85-86. Reprinted by permission of the author.

## GIVING SAVES FROM SELFISHNESS

In *Money the Acid Test,* David McConaughy quotes an unknown writer who says that whereas spending protects from miserliness, saving from wastefulness, and counting from dishonesty, it is giving that saves from selfishness. John Oxenham says that love's prerogative is not only to give but to give again, and then to give still again. To do this kind of giving, most families will have to take the tithe off the top, instead of the bottom.

Robert J. Hastings, *How To Manage Your Money* (Nashville: Broadman Press, 1965), pp. 87-88. Reprinted by permission of the author.

## GIVING SAVES US FROM OURSELVES

Frequently the giver is the biggest receiver, for in giving we save ourselves *from ourselves.* Studio technicians were testing different sound effects to represent the clanging of chains on the ankles of a prisoner. The rattle of clinking coins was finally selected as the most authentic. Likewise, money can act like chains on our hearts, as well as to sound like money on our feet.

Robert J. Hastings, *How To Manage Your Money* (Nashville: Broadman Press, 1965), p. 87. Reprinted by permission of the author.

## MOTIVES FOR GIVING

In giving, some do so out of a sense of duty. They feel it is their responsibility as a member of the congregation to "do their part," as they would in a club. Others give out of hope for reward or recognition, and others because they feel under pressure. A few may give out of fear, apprehensive lest God punish them in some way in the form of illness, accident, or other misfortune. Some give out of pity. But the noblest motive is Christian love, which doesn't wait to be flattered, pressured, or begged. Love assumes the initiative, takes the first step, seeks the altars which need its gifts. This is the essence of Christianity —loving, seeking, searching, weeping, finding, giving, saving, lifting, healing.

Robert J. Hastings, *How To Manage Your Money* (Nashville: Broadman Press, 1965), pp. 85-86. Reprinted by permission of the author.

## THE REASON WE CAN'T FIND SATISFACTION IN WEALTH ALONE

Do you remember what Carlyle said? "Not all the financiers, upholsterers and confectioners joined together in a stock company can make one shoe-black happy for more than an hour or so, because the shoe-black has an immortal soul in him quite other than his stomach, which would require the infinite universe to fulfil." The reason why we can't find lasting satisfaction in earthly treasure is not that the world is made too big for us but that we are made too big for it. The infinite within us will not let us be satisfied with finite things.

J. Wallace Hamilton, *Ride the Wild Horses!* (Westwood, N.J.: Fleming H. Revell Company, 1952), p. 59. Reprinted by permission of the publisher.

# ... ABOUT WHAT MONEY CAN DO

Albert Schweitzer has said that while money will not bring about the Kingdom of God, yet the Kingdom of God cannot be achieved without money.

A. Leonard Griffith, *God and His People,* (New York and Nashville: Abingdon Press, 1960), p. 68. Reprinted by permission of the publisher.

> I care for riches, to make gifts
> To friends, or lead a sick man back to health
> With ease and plenty. Else small aid is wealth
> For daily gladness; once a man be done
> With hunger, rich and poor are all as one.
>
> Euripides

Herschel H. Hobbs in *Studying Life and Work Lessons,* July, August, September, 1969 (Nashville: Convention Press, 1969), p. 56. Used by permission.

## HOW TO LAY UP TREASURES IN HEAVEN

How does one lay up treasures in heaven: Dr. Pat Neff once said that the only way to get treasures into heaven is to invest them in things that are going to heaven—in people. Material, temporal things are not going to heaven—only men, women, boys and girls.

Herschel H. Hobbs, *Studying Life and Work Lessons,* July, August, September, 1969 (Nashville: Convention Press, 1969), pp. 57-58. Used by permission.

## THE RIGHT USE OF MONEY

... money, rightly made and rightly used, may be a source of endless good. How often we hear someone misquote Paul by saying, "Money is the root of all evil." Paul said no such thing. He had far too much intelligence to say anything so silly.

Money can feed the hungry and clothe the naked. Money can build schools, colleges, and universities. Money can erect churches to the glory of God. I know that I can take a dollar and use it in such a fashion as to make the eagle upon it turn vulture to tear at somebody's heart. But I can also take that same dollar and so use it that the eagle upon it will become a mockingbird to make music in somebody's soul. Money rightly used is a means of endless good.

Clovis G. Chappell, *Ten Rules for Living* (New York and Nashville: Abingdon Press, 1938), p. 33. Reprinted by permission of the publisher.

## SERVING GOD WITH MAMMON

One cannot serve both God and mammon. But he can serve God with mammon. To do so is to lay up treasures in heaven and to be used in bringing the kingdom of God in the hearts of men.

Herschel H. Hobbs, *Studying Life and Work Lessons,* July, August, September, 1969 (Nashville: Convention Press, 1969), p. 60. Used by permission.

As the love of money is the root of all evil, so the love of what money can do is a root of all kinds of righteousness, peace, and good will in the world.

It is easy to know when to stop giving to the Lord's work; just give till the Master stops giving to you.

Anonymous.

Money is an article which may be used as a universal passport to everywhere except Heaven, and as a universal provider of everything except happiness.

Anonymous.

By doing good with his money a man, as it were, stamps the image of God upon it, and makes it pass current for the merchandise of heaven.

John Rutledge.

Money is another pair of legs and, lo! it can go where otherwise we could never go, walking amid the need of China today or ministering in India and the islands of the sea. Money is another pair of hands and it can carry burdens that our own fingers cannot touch in our community, our nation, and around the world. Money is another pair of vocal cords and it can speak where our voice could not be heard, teaching and preaching where in personal presence we may never go. What a man does with his money he is in a real sense doing himself.

Harry Emerson Fosdick

Quoted in the bulletin of the First Baptist Church, Altus, Oklahoma.

## GIVING IS AN ACT OF WORSHIP

Have you ever thought of giving as an act of worship? Have you noticed that the order of worship for Sunday morning includes a section entitled "Worship in Giving?" Well, giving although it seems a little "earthly" is indeed an act of worship.

A seven-year-old girl was visiting a neighborhood friend. When grace was said at the table she was mystified. "Why did you do that?" she asked. "We thank God for our food," she was told. "Oh," the seven-year-old responded, "we pay for ours."

And so do we all "pay for ours." Yet we worship God because we know how much He gives "beyond all we could ask or think," or pay for with our toil.

We give in gratitude and in reverence before the mystery of God's bounty. We do not respond to the summons, "O come let us worship and bow down, let us kneel before the Lord, our Maker," because we are forced. Rather we respond because we are aware how much is ours through the goodness of God. The wealth of the good earth and the gentle conspiracy of nature nourishing its fruition are gifts beyond anything money can buy. The pageantry of the seasons that mocks the attire of kings and the grace of our Lord Jesus Christ are gifts beyond measure too.

So we worship and adore the living God with reverent words. But sometimes we forget that worship involves more than words spoken with feeling in the sanctuary or at the table. Words are only symbols without substance unless they involve the commitment of ourselves and our possessions to the God we worship.

At the heart of worship is self-giving in gratitude for God's gifts that money cannot buy. And worship does not end until the giving begins. What is more life's wholeness awaits graciousness in giving.

Walt Whitman once wrote, "The ignorant man is demented with the madness of owning things." The wise man is made whole with the divine madness of bestowing his wealth on the altars of the Kingdom of God.

Someone has penned these pertinent lines:

> Give a proportion of thy gains to God,
> And sanctify thy income. Set apart
> A well-considered portion cheerfully
> As thy thank-offering for His bounteous love.

Giving is an act of worship. How do you worship? in WORD or DEED or BOTH?

Larry Baker, Pastor, Parkview Baptist Church, Monroe, Louisiana. Used by permission.

## MAKING MONEY OUR SERVANT

I suppose some people might think I am also taking a risk by investing some money in religious activities when I could be spending it in a dozen other ways. I have a pretty strong feeling about the danger of money and the desire for wealth. Money has a strong appeal to almost everyone, and the love of it can creep up on us until it takes command of our lives. There are so many delectable things we would like to buy, so many urgent needs. But money is a hard taskmaster. It demands its pound of flesh and takes its toll in blood, sweat, and tears.

Money should properly be our servant, and each of us needs something to prevent it from becoming our master. By developing the habit of giving our money to religious causes and various other worthy causes, we can tear ourselves loose from our eager taskmaster and build stronger characters. It won't do to tell ourselves that a good portion of our tax money goes to good causes. When we pay our taxes we are doing something required of us, and nothing in that will strengthen our character. When we give our money voluntarily, we are doing something we are not required to do, and we grow through the experience.

W. Maxey Jarman, *A Businessman Looks at the Bible* (Westwood, N.J.: Fleming H. Revell Company, 1965), pp. 43-44. Reprinted by permission of the publisher.

# . . . ABOUT WHAT MONEY CANNOT DO

## WEALTH ALONE DOES NOT BRING HAPPINESS

It is said that Cecil Rhodes looked with envy on General William Booth of the Salvation Army. Asked once if he were happy, Rhodes replied: "Happy? I happy? Good God, no! I would give all that I possess to believe what that old man believes."

*The Life and Work Lesson Annual,* 1969-70 (Nashville: Convention Press, 1969), p. 223. Used by permission.

Make money your God, and it will plague you like the devil.

Henry Fielding.

*Vincentio, Duke of Vienna, to Claudio:*

> If thou art rich, thou art poor;
> For, like an ass whose back with ingots bows,
> Thou bear'st thy heavy riches but a journey,
> And death unloads thee.

William Shakespeare, *Measure for Measure,* III, 1.

> To purchase heaven, has gold the power?
> Can gold remove the mortal hour?
> In life can love be bought with gold?
> Are friendships pleasures to be sold?
> No—all that's worth a wish—a thought,
> Fair virtue gives unbrid'd, unbought,
> Cease then on trash thy hopes to bind,
> Let nobler views engage thy mind.

Samuel Johnson, quoted by Herschel H. Hobbs, in *Studying Life and Work Lessons,* July, August, September, 1969 (Nashville: Convention Press, 1969), p. 56. Used by permission.

He that is of the opinion that money will do everything, may well be suspected of doing everything for money.

Benjamin Franklin.

## INVESTING IN ETERNAL THINGS

An ancient custom was to place a man's treasures in his tomb to be used by him in the world beyond. Jesus said that one should send his treasures on ahead so that they will be there when he arrives. If his heart has been deposited in eternal things, he should invest·his treasures in them also. Only such values are legal tender in heaven.

Herschel H. Hobbs, *Studying Life and Work Lessons,* July, August, September, 1969 (Nashville: Convention Press, 1969), p. 58. Used by permission.

Ill fares the land, to hastening ills a prey,
When wealth accumulates, and men decay.

Oliver Goldsmith, quoted by Herschel H. Hobbs in *Studying Life and Work Lessons,* July, August, September, 1969 (Nashville: Convention Press, 1968), p. 56. Used by permission.

## MONEY IS WHAT YOU MAKE IT

Dug from the mountainside, washed from the glen,
Servant am I or master of men.
Steal me, I curse you;
Earn me, I bless you;
Grasp me and hoard me, a fiend shall possess you;
Live for me, die for me.
Covet me, take me,
Angel or devil, I am what you make me.

Arthur Guiterman, quoted by Fred M. Wood in *Bible Truth in Person* (Nashville: Broadman Press, 1956), p. 84. Reprinted by permission of the author.

# ... ABOUT THE RESULTS OF STEWARDSHIP

## GIVING

Go give to the needy
Sweet charity's bread,
For "giving is living,"
The angel said,
But must I keep giving
Again and again?
My peevish and pitiless
Curt answer ran.
"Oh, no," said the angel,
Piercing me through,
"Just give till the Master
Stops giving to you."

Author Unknown.

It pays to serve God, but it doesn't pay to serve God because it pays.

R. G. LeTourneau.

There is no portion of our time that is our time, and the rest God's; there is no portion of money that is our money, and the rest God's money. It is all His; He made it all, gives it all, and He has simply trusted it to us for His service. A servant has two purses, the master's and his own, but we have only one.

Alolphe Monod.

## SUFFICIENCY IN GOD: GOD IS NOT GOING BROKE

A friend who had spent years of his dynamic life in a tortured drive for wealth made his "pile." Then financial disaster stripped him of all his possessions, but he became a man instead of a machine. He found Christ as Saviour and Lord of his life. With tears of gratitude he told me: "Now I have all that's worth wanting. And tomorrow? I don't even worry about that now! I've found Paul's words to be the most sensible truth of my life: 'My God will supply every need of yours according to his riches in glory in Christ Jesus.' And I know that God is not going broke!"

*The Life and Work Lesson Annual,* 1969-1970 (Nashville: Convention Press, 1969), p. 295. Used by permission.

Riches are the least worthy gifts which God can give man. What are they to God's word, to bodily gifts, such as beauty and health, or to the gifts of the mind, such as understanding, skill, wisdom! Yet men toil for them day and night, and take no rest. Therefore God commonly gives riches to foolish people, to whom he gives nothing else.

Martin Luther.

If in carnal wealth, how much more in spiritual does God love a cheerful giver?

St. Augustine: "Of the Catechizing of the Unlearned"

It is possible to give without loving, but it is impossible to love without giving.

Richard Braunstein.

All good things of this world are no further good than as they are of use; and whatever we may heap up to give to others, we enjoy only as much as we can make useful to ourselves and others, and no more.

Daniel Defoe.

A beneficent person is like a fountain watering the earth

and spreading fertility; it is therefore more delightful and more honorable to give than to receive.

Epicurus.

The fact is, we get what we give, no more, no less, and let us remember that every time we put up a fence we shut out more than we shut in.

John Herman Randall.

The value of the gift is sometimes determined by what the giver has left.

Giving is the secret of a healthy life. Not necessarily money, but whatever a man has of encouragement and sympathy and understanding.

John D. Rockefeller, Jr.

> That gift of his, from God descended.
> Ah! friend, what gift of man's does not?

Robert Browning, "Christmas Eve," Canto XVI.

It is what we give up, not what we lay up, that adds to our lasting store.

Hosea Ballou.

## GIVING THROUGH THE CHURCH: AN ATTEMPT TO REDEEM THE TOTAL MAN

And right here is the reason many responsible Christian families give through and in the name of their churches. All the missionary, educational, and benevolent work of a church should aim at redeeming the total man, of making him a responsible citizen in society as well as a member of the kingdom of God. So Christian families want not only to meet the physical needs of others but to give in the name of Christ to the end that the recipient's whole life is revolutionized.

Robert J. Hastings, *How To Manage Your Money* (Nashville: Broadman Press, 1965), p. 89. Used with permission of the author.

## AMOUNT OF MONEY GIVEN

The average American family gave only one cent out of each dollar during 1963, and we have little reason to believe the average is much higher now. As we shuffle the family dollar, we pitch a penny crumb and call it "giving."

Robert J. Hastings, *How To Manage Your Money* (Nashville: Broadman Press, 1965), p. 84. Used with permission of the author.

## THE DIFFERENCE IN SUPPORTING GOD'S ENTERPRISE AND SHARING IN IT

The Church demeans itself if it plays the role of a beggar and simply parades its needs by means of statistics or emotional stories in the hope that its members will be impressed and conscience-stricken and stirred to a point of generosity. The Church is not a charity organization that depends on a generous public to keep it going. The Church is an enterprise, the greatest enterprise in history, God's own enterprise for the salvation of the world. Never has any enterprise so stood the test of time or so proved its worth or paid richer dividends in all that it has accomplished for the life of mankind. We are not invited to support God's enterprise but to share in it, to be partners with all who have served Christ through the centuries and all who serve Him in the world today.

A. Leonard Griffith, *This Is Living* (Nashville: Abingdon Press, 1966), p. 153. Reprinted by permission of the publisher.

## MONEY SYMBOLIZES THE OFFERING OF SELF

Money symbolizes the offering of self because money most authentically represents the self. Money is congealed life, our own sinew, time, labour and ability reduced to negotiable form.

What we do with our money we do in a very real sense with ourselves.

A. Leonard Griffith, *This Is Living* (Nashville: Abingdon Press, 1966), p. 155. Reprinted by permission of the publisher.